Pythagoras
and the
Delphic Mysteries

Contents: Greece in the Sixth Century; Years of Travel; The Temple of Delphi; The Order and the Doctrine; Marriage of Pythagoras; Revolution at Croton; The Master's End; The School and its Destiny.

Edouard Schure

ISBN 1-56459-515-3

" Know thyself, and thou wilt know the Universe and the Gods."—*Inscription on the Temple of Delphi.*

Evolution is the law of Life,
Number is the law of the Universe,
Unity is the law of God.

CONTENTS

PYTHAGORAS

CHAPTER I

GREECE IN THE SIXTH CENTURY

THE soul of Orpheus had passed like a divine meteor across the troubled heavens of a new-born Greece. When the meteor had disappeared, the land was again wrapt in darkness. After a series of revolutions, the tyrants of Thrace committed his books to the flames, overthrew his temples and drove away his disciples. The Greek kings and numerous cities followed this example, more jealous of their unbridled licence than of that justice which is the source of pure doctrine. They were determined to efface his very memory, to leave no sign of his existence, and they succeeded so well, that, a few centuries after his death, a portion of Greece even doubted whether he had ever lived. It was in vain that the initiates kept alive his tradition for over a thousand years; in vain that Pythagoras and Plato spoke of him as divine; the sophists and the rhetoricians saw in him no more than a legend regarding the origin of music. Even at the present time, savants stoutly deny the existence of Orpheus, basing their assertion on the fact that neither Homer nor Hesiod mentioned his name. The silence of these poets, however, is fully explained by the interdict under which the local government had placed the great initiator. The disciples of Orpheus lost no opportunity of rallying all the powers under the supreme authority of the temple of Delphi, and never tired of repeating that the differences arising between the divers states of Greece must be laid before the council of the Amphictyons. This was displeasing to demagogues and tyrants alike. Homer, who probably received his initiation in the sanctuary of Tyre, and whose mythology is the poetical translation of the theology of Sankoniaton, Homer the Ionian might very well have known nothing of the Dorian Orpheus whose tradition was kept all the more secret as it was the more exposed to persecution. As regards Hesiod, who was born near Parnassus, he must have known the name and doctrine of Orpheus through the temple at Delphi; but silence was imposed on him by his initiators, and that for good reasons.

And yet Orpheus was living in his work, in his

disciples, and even in those who denied his very existence. What is this work, where can the soul of his life be sought? In the ferocious, military oligarchy of Sparta, where science was despised, ignorance erected into a system, and brutality exacted as being the complement of courage? In those implacable wars of Messenia in which the Spartans were seen persecuting a neighbouring people to the point of extermination, and these Romans of Greece preparing for the Tarpeian rock and the bleeding laurels of the Capitol by hurling the heroic Aristomenes, the defender of his country, into an abyss? Or should it rather be sought in the turbulent democracy of Athens, ever ready to convert itself into a tyranny? Or in the praetorian guard of Pisistratus, or the dagger of Harmodius and Aristogiton, concealed under a myrtle branch? Or in the many towns and cities of Hellas, of greater Greece and Asia Minor, of which Athens and Sparta offer us two opposing types? Is it in all these envious, these jealous democracies and tyrannies ever ready to tear one another into pieces?—No; the soul of Greece is not there. It is in her temples, her mysteries and their initiates. It is in the sanctuary of Jupiter at Olympia, of Juno at Argos, of Ceres at Eleusis; it reigns over Athens with Minerva, it sheds its beams over Delphi with

Apollo, who penetrates every temple with his light. Here is the centre of Hellenic life, the heart and brain of Greece. Here come for instruction poets who translate sublime truth into living images for the masses, sages who propagate these truths in subtle dialectics. The spirit of Orpheus is felt wherever beats the heart of immortal Greece. We find it in poetry and gymnastic contests, in the Delphic and Olympian games, a glorious project instituted by the successors of the Master with the object of drawing nearer together and uniting the twelve Greek tribes. We are brought into direct contact with it in the court of the Amphictyons, in that assembly of the great initiates, a supreme, arbitrary tribunal, which met at Delphi, a mighty centre of justice and concord, in which alone Greece recovered her unity in times of heroism and abnegation.[1]

And yet Greece in the time of Orpheus; her intellect, an unsullied, temple-guarded doctrine; her soul, a plastic religion; and her body, a lofty

---

[1] The *Amphictyonic oath* of the allied peoples gives some idea of the greatness and social might of this institution: "We swear that we will never overthrow Amphictyonic towns, never, during either peace or war, prevent them from obtaining whatever is necessary for their needs. Should any power dare to attempt this, we will march against it and destroy its towns. Should impious hands remove the offerings of the temple of Apollo, we swear that we will use our feet, our arms, our voice, and all our strength against them and their accomplices."

court of justice with Delphi as its centre, had begun to decline early in the seventh century. The orders sent out from Delphi were no longer respected, the sacred territories were violated. The race of men of mighty inspiration had disappeared, the intellectual and moral tone of the temples deteriorated; the priests sold themselves to politicians. From that time the Mysteries themselves became corrupted.

The general aspect of Greece had changed. The old sacerdotal and agricultural royalty was succeeded either by tyranny pure and simple, by military aristocracy, or by anarchical democracy. The temples had become powerless to check the threatening ruin. A new helper was needed. It was therefore necessary to popularize esoteric teaching. To enable the thought of Orpheus to live and expand in all its beauty, the knowledge of the temples must pass over to the lay classes. Accordingly, under different disguises, it penetrated the brains of civil legislators, the schools of the poets, and the porticoes of the philosophers. The latter felt in their teachings the very necessity Orpheus had recognized in religion, that of two doctrines: the one public and the other secret, manifesting the same truth in different degree and form, and suited to the development of the pupil. This evolution gave Greece her three great centuries of artistic creation and intellectual splendour. It permitted the Orphic thought, at once the initial impulse and the ideal synthesis of Greece, to concentrate its entire light and radiate it over the whole world, before her political edifice, undermined by internal dissensions, tottered beneath the power of Macedonia and finally crumbled away under the iron hand of Rome.

Many contributed to the evolution we are speaking of. It brought out natural philosophers like Thales, legislators like Solon, poets like Pindar, and heroes like Epaminondas. It had also a recognized head, an initiate of the very first rank, a sovereign, organizing, creating intelligence. Pythagoras is the master of lay as Orpheus is the master of sacerdotal Greece. He translates and continues the religious thought of his predecessor, applying it to the new times. His translation, however, is a creation, for he co-ordinates the Orphic inspirations into a complete system, gives scientific proof of them in his teachings and moral proof in his institute of education, and in the Pythagorean order which survived him.

Although appearing in the full light of historical times, Pythagoras has come down to us as almost a legendary character. The main reason for this is the terrible persecution of which he was the victim in Sicily, and which cost so many of his followers their lives. Some were crushed to death beneath the ruins of their burning schools, others died of hunger in temples. The Master's memory and teaching were only perpetuated by such survivors as were able to escape into Greece. Plato, at great trouble and cost, obtained through Archytas a manuscript of the Master, who, it must be mentioned, never transferred to writing his esoteric teachings except under symbols and secret characters. His real work, like that of all reformers, was effected by oral instruction. The essence of the system, however, comes down to us in the *Golden Verses* of Lysis, the commentary of Hierocles, fragments of Philolaus and in the Timaeus of Plato, which contains the cosmogony of Pythagoras. To sum up, the writers of antiquity are full of the spirit of the Croton philosopher. They never tire of relating anecdotes depicting his wisdom and beauty, his marvellous power over men. The Neoplatonists of Alexandria, the Gnostics, and even the early Fathers of the Church quote him as an authority. These are precious witnesses through whom may be felt continually vibrating that mighty wave of enthusiasm the great personality of Pythagoras succeeded in communicating to Greece, the final eddies of which were still to be felt eight hundred years after his death.

His teaching, regarded from above, and unlocked with the keys of comparative esoterism, affords a magnificent whole, the different parts of which are bound together by one fundamental conception. In it we find a rational reproduction of the esoteric teaching of India and Egypt, which he illumined with Hellenic simplicity and clearness, giving it a stronger sentiment and a clearer idea of human liberty.

At the same time and at different parts of the globe, mighty reformers were popularizing similar doctrines. Lao-Tse in China was emerging from the esoterism of Fo-Hi; the last Buddha Sakya-Mouni was preaching on the banks of the Ganges; in Italy, the Etrurian priesthood sent to Rome an initiate possessed of the Sibylline books. This was King Numa, who, by wise institutions, attempted to check the threatening ambition of the Roman Senate. It was not by chance that these reformers appeared simultaneously among such different peoples. Their diverse missions had one common end in view. They prove that, at certain periods, one identical spiritual current passes mysteriously through the whole of humanity. Whence comes it? It has its source in that divine world, far away from human vision, but of which prophets and seers are the envoys and witnesses.

Pythagoras crossed the whole of the ancient world before giving his message to Greece. He saw Africa and Asia, Memphis and Babylon, along with their methods of initiation and political life. His own troubled life resembles a ship driving through a storm, pursuing its course, with sails unfurled, a symbol of strength and calmness in the midst of the furious elements. His teachings convey the impression of a cool fragrant night after the bitter fire and passion of an angry, blood-stained day. They call to mind the beauty of the firmament unrolling, by degrees, its sparkling archipelagoes and ethereal harmonies over the head of the seer.

And now we will attempt to set forth both his life and his teaching apart from the obscurities of legend and the prejudices of the schools alike.

CHAPTER II

AT the beginning of the sixth century before our era, Samos was one of the most flourishing islands of Ionia. Its harbour fronted the violet peaks of a slumbering Asia Minor, the abode of luxury and charm. The town was situated on a wide bay with verdant coasts, and retreated, tier upon tier, up the mountain in the form of an amphitheatre, itself lying at the foot of a promontory on which stood the temple of Neptune. It was dominated by the colonnades of a magnificent palace, the abode of the tyrant Polycrates. After depriving Samos of her liberty he had given the island all the lustre of art and Asiatic splendour. Courtesans from Lesbos had, at his bidding, taken up their abode in a neighbouring palace to which they invited the young men and maidens of the town. At these *fêtes* they taught them the most refined voluptuousness, accompanied with music, dancing and feasting. Anacreon, on the invitation of Polycrates, was transported to Samos in a trireme with purple sails and gilded masts; the poet, a goblet of chased

silver in his hand, sang before this high court of
pleasure his languishing odes. The good fortune
of Polycrates had become proverbial throughout
Greece. He had as a friend the Pharaoh Amasis
who often warned him to be on his guard against
such unbroken fortune, and above all not to pride
himself on it. Polycrates answered the Egyptian
monarch's advice by flinging his ring into the sea.
" This sacrifice I offer unto the gods," he said.
The following day a fisherman brought back to the
tyrant the precious jewel, which he had found in
the belly of a fish. When the Pharaoh heard of
this, he said he would break off his friendship with
Polycrates, for such insolent good fortune would
draw down on him the vengeance of the gods.—
Whatever we may think of the anecdote, the end of
Polycrates was a tragic one. One of his satraps
enticed him into a neighbouring province, tortured
him to death, and ordered his body to be fastened
to a cross on Mount Mycale. And so, one evening as the blood-red orb of the sun was sinking in
the west, the inhabitants of Samos saw the corpse
of their tyrant, crucified on a promontory in sight
of the island over which he had reigned in glory
and abandonment.

To return to the beginning of Polycrates' reign.
One star-lit night a young man was seated in a

wood of agnus castus, with its glimmering foliage, not far from the temple of Juno, the Doric front of which was bathed in the rays of the moon, whose light added to the mystic majesty of the building. A papyrus roll, containing a song of Homer, had slipped to the ground, and lay at his feet. His meditation, begun at twilight, was continued into the silence of the night. The sun had long ago disappeared beneath the horizon, but its flaming disc still danced in unreal presence before the eyes of the young dreamer. His thoughts had wandered far from the world of visible things.

Pythagoras was the son of a wealthy jeweller of Samos and of a woman named Parthenis. The Pythoness of Delphi, when consulted during a journey by the young married couple, had promised them : " a son who would be useful to all men and throughout all time." The oracle had sent them to Sidon, in Phoenicia, so that the predestined son might be conceived, formed, and born far from the disturbing influences of his own land. Even before his birth the wonderful child, in the moon of love, had been fervently consecrated to the worship of Apollo by his parents. The child was born; and when he was a year old his mother, acting on advice already received from the priest of Delphi, bore him away to the temple of Adonaï, in a valley of Lebanon. Here the high priest had given him his blessing and the family returned to Samos. The child of Parthenis was very beautiful and gentle, calm and sedate. Intellectual passion alone gleamed from his eyes, giving a secret energy to his actions. Far from opposing, his parents had encouraged him in his precocious leaning towards the study of wisdom. He had been left free to confer with the priests of Samos and the savants who were beginning to establish in Ionia schools in which the principles of natural philosophy were taught. At the age of eighteen he had attended the classes of Hermodamas of Samos, at twenty those of Pherecydes at Syros; he had even conferred with Thales and Anaximander at Miletus. These masters had opened out new horizons, though none had satisfied him. In their contradictory teachings he tried to discover the bond and synthesis, the unity of the great whole. The son of Parthenis had now reached one of those crises in which the mind, over-excited by the contradictions of things, concentrates all its faculties in one supreme effort to obtain a glimpse of the end, to find a path leading to the sun of truth, to the centre of life.

Throughout that glorious night Pythagoras fixed his gaze on the earth, the temple, and the starry heavens in turn. Demeter, the earth-mother, the

Nature whose secrets he wished to pierce, was there, beneath and around him. He inhaled her powerful emanations, felt the invincible attraction which enchained him, the thinking atom, to her bosom, an inseparable part of herself. The sages he had consulted had said to him : " It is from her that all springs. Nothing comes from nothing. The soul comes from water, or fire, or from both. This subtle emanation of the elements issues from them only to return. Eternal Nature is blind and inflexible, resign thyself to her fatal laws. The only merit thou wilt have will be that thou knowest them, and art resigned thereto."

Then he looked at the firmament and the fiery letters formed by the constellations in the unfathomable depths of space. These letters must have a meaning. For if the infinitely small, the movement of atoms, has its *raison d'être*, why not also the infinitely great, the widely scattered stars, whose grouping represents the body of the universe? Yes; each of these worlds has its own law; all move together according to number and in supreme harmony. But who will ever decipher the alphabet of the stars? The priests of Juno had said to him : " This is the heaven of the gods, which was before the earth. Thy soul comes therefrom. Pray to them, that it may mount again to heaven."

These meditations were interrupted by a voluptuous chant, coming from a garden on the banks of the Imbrasus. The lascivious voices of the Lesbian women, in languishing strains, were heard accompanying the music of the cithara, responded to in the Bacchic airs chanted by the youths. Suddenly other cries, piercing and mournful, from the direction of the harbour, mingled with these voices. They were the cries of rebels whom Polycrates was embarking to sell as slaves in Asia. They were being struck with nail-studded thongs, to compel them to crouch beneath the pontoons of the rowers. Their shrieks and blasphemous cries died away in the night and silence reigned over all.

A painful thrill ran through the young man's frame; he checked it in an attempt to regain possession of himself. The problem lay before him, more pressing and poignant than before. Earth said: *Fatality*. Heaven said: *Providence*. Mankind, between the two, replied: *Madness! Pain! Slavery!* In the depths of his own nature, however, the future adept heard an invincible voice replying to the chains of earth and the flaming heavens with the cry: *Liberty!* Who were right; sages, or priests, the wretched or the mad, or was it himself? In reality all these voices spoke the truth, each triumphed in its own sphere, but none gave

2

up to him its *raison d'être*. The three worlds all
existed, unchangeable as the heart of Demeter, the
light of the constellations and the human breast,
but only the one who could find agreement between
them and the law of their equilibrium would be
truly wise; he alone would be in possession of
divine knowledge and capable of aiding mankind.
It was in the synthesis of the three worlds that the
secret of the *Kosmos* lay!

As he gave utterance to this discovery he had just
made, Pythagoras rose to his feet. His eager
glance was fixed on the Doric façade of the temple;
the majestic building seemed transfigured beneath
Diana's chaste beams. There he believed that
he saw the ideal image of the world and the solu-
tion of the problem he was seeking. The base,
columns, architrave, and triangular pediment suddenly represented, in his eyes, the triple nature of
man and the universe, of the microcosm and the
macrocosm crowned by divine unity, itself a trinity.
The Kosmos, controlled and penetrated by God,
formed

"The sacred Quaternion, the source of Nature;
whose cause is eternal."[1]

Yes, here concealed in these geometrical lines
was the key of the universe, the science of numbers,

---

[1] *The Golden Verses of Pythagoras.*

the ternary law regulating the constitution of beings, and the septenary law that governs their evolution. Pythagoras saw the worlds move through space in accordance with the rhythm and harmony of the sacred numbers. He saw the balance of earth and heaven of which human liberty holds control; the three worlds, the natural, the human, and the divine, sustaining and determining one another, and playing the universal drama in a double—ascending and descending—movement. He divided the spheres of the invisible enveloping the visible world and ever animating it; finally, he conceived of the purification and liberation of man, on this globe, by triple initiation. All this he saw, along with his life and work, in an instantaneous flash of illumination, with the absolute certainty of the spirit brought face to face with Truth. Now he must prove by Reason what his pure Intelligence had obtained from the Absolute, and this needed a human life, it was the task of a Hercules.

Where could he find the knowledge necessary to bring such a labour to a successful issue? Neither the songs of Homer, nor the sages of Ionia, nor the temples of Greece would suffice.

The spirit of Pythagoras, which had suddenly found wings, began to plunge into his past life, into his mist-enveloped birth and his mother's mysterious love. Childhood's memory returned to him with striking clearness. He recalled the fact that his mother had carried him in her arms, when only a babe of twelve months, to the temple of Adonaï, in a vale of Lebanon. He saw himself again as a child, clinging to the neck of Parthenis, with mighty forests and mountains all around, whilst the river formed a waterfall close by. She was standing on a terrace shaded with giant cedars. In front of her stood a majestic-looking, white-bearded priest, smiling on the mother and child as he uttered grave-sounding words the little one did not understand. Often had his mother brought back to his mind the strange utterance of the hierophant of Adonaï: " O woman of Ionia, thy son shall be great in wisdom; but remember that, though the Greeks still possess the science *of the gods*, the knowledge *of God* can no longer be found elsewhere than in Egypt." These words came back to him along with his mother's smile, the old man's beautiful face, and the distant murmur of the waterfall dominated by the priest's voice, with that magnificent scenery all around, like the dream of another life. For the first time he guessed the meaning of the oracle. He had indeed heard of the wonderful knowledge of Egyptian priests and their dreadful mysteries, though he thought he could do without it all. Now he understood that he needed this "science of God," to penetrate to the very heart of nature, and that he could find it only in the temples of Egypt. It was the gentle Parthenis who, with maternal instinct, had prepared him for this work, and borne him as an offering to the sovereign God! From this moment he made up his mind to go to Egypt, and there undergo initiation.

Polycrates prided himself on being the protector of philosophers as well as of poets. He willingly gave Pythagoras a letter of recommendation to Pharaoh Amasis, who introduced him to the priests of Memphis. The latter were opposed to receiving him, and were induced to consent only with the utmost difficulty. Egyptian sages distrusted Greeks, whom they charged with being fickle and inconstant. They did all they could to discourage the young Samian. The novice, however, submitted with unfaltering patience and courage to the delays and tests imposed on him. He knew beforehand that he would only attain to knowledge by entirely mastering his will throughout his entire being. His initiation under the pontificate of Sonchis the high priest lasted twenty-two years. All the trials and temptations, the soul-rending dread and ecstatic joy pased through by Hermes, the initiate of Isis, even to the apparent, or cataleptic death of the adept and his resurrection in the light of Osiris, were experienced by Pythagoras, so that he now realized, not as a vain theory, but as something lived through, the doctrine of the Logos-Light, or of the universal Word, and that of human evolution through seven planetary cycles. At each step of this giddy ascent the tests became more formidable. A hundred times the risk of death was incurred, especially if one's object was to gain control over occult forces, and attain to the dangerous practice of magic and theurgy.   Like all great men, Pythagoras believed in his star. No path that led to knowledge disheartened him, the fear of death could not check him, for he saw life beyond. When the Egyptian priests had recognized that he possessed extraordinary strength of soul and that impersonal passion for wisdom, which is the rarest thing in the world, they opened out to him the treasures of their experience. Whilst with them he daily improved, and became filled with divine knowledge. He mastered sacred mathematics and the science of numbers, or universal principles, which he formulated anew and made the centre of his system. The severity of the Egyptian discipline in the temples also impressed on him the prodigious power of the human will when wisely trained and exercised, the endless applications, both to body and to soul, that can be made of it. " The science of numbers and the art of will-power," said the priests of Memphis, " are the two keys of magic; they open up all the gates of the universe." It was in Egypt that Pythagoras obtained that view from above, which allows of one seeing the spheres of life and the sciences in concentric order, and understanding the *involution* of the spirit into matter by universal creation, and its *evolution* or re-ascent towards unity by way of that individual creation called the development of a consciousness.

Pythagoras had reached the summit of Egyptian priesthood, and was perhaps thinking of returning to Greece, when war, with all its misery, burst upon the valley of the Nile, carrying away the initiate of Osiris in another direction. The despots of Asia had long been meditating the ruin of Egypt. Their repeated attacks had failed, for centuries past, before the wisdom of the Egyptian institutions, the power of the priesthood, and the energy of the Pharaohs. But the refuge of the science of Hermes, the kingdom from time immemorial, was not to remain for ever. Cambyses, son of the conqueror of Babylon, descended on Egypt with his innumerable hosts, famished as clouds of locusts,

and put an end to the institution of the Pharaohs,
the origin of which was lost in the night of time.
In the eyes of the sages this was a catastrophe for
the whole world. Hitherto Egypt had sheltered
Europe against Asia. Her protecting influence
still extended over the whole basin of the Mediter-
ranean, by means of the temples of Phoenicia,
Greece, and Etruria, with which the high Egyptian
priesthood were in constant connection. This ram-
part once overthrown, the Bull, with lowered head,
was about to burst upon the land of Greece. Pythagoras saw Cambyses invade Egypt, he may have
beheld the Persian despot, worthy scion of the
crowned villains of Nineveh and Babylon, plunder
the temples of Memphis and Thebes, and destroy
that of Ammon. He may have seen the Pharaoh
Psammitichus brought in chains before Cambyses,
placed on a mound, and surrounded by the priests,
the principal families, and the royal court. He may
have witnessed the Pharaoh's daughter, clad in rags
and followed by all her maids of honour similarly
demeaned, the royal prince and two thousand young
men, brought forward, bit in mouth and bridle on
neck, before being beheaded; the Pharaoh Psammitichus, choking back his sobs before the frightful
scene, and the infamous Cambyses, seated on his
throne, gloating over the anguish of his vanquished

enemy. Cruel though instructive this lesson of history after those of science! What a picture of the animal nature let loose in man, culminating in this monster of despotism who tramples everything under foot, and, by his horrible apotheosis, imposes on humanity the reign of a most implacable destiny!

Cambyses had Pythagoras taken to Babylon, with a portion of the Egyptian priesthood, and kept him within the gates.[1] This colossal city, which Aristotle compares to a country surrounded by walls, offered at that time an immense field for observation. Ancient Babel, the great prostitute of the Hebrew prophets, was more than ever, after the Persian conquest, a pandemonium of nations, tongues, and religions, in whose midst Asiatic despotism raised aloft its dizzy tower. According to Persian tradition, its foundation dates back to the legendary Semiramis. She it is who was said to have constructed the monster *enceinte*, over fifty miles in circumference: the Imgur-Bel, its walls on which two chariots ran abreast, its superimposed terraces, massive palaces with polychrome reliefs, temples supported on stone elephants and surmounted by many-coloured dragons. There had followed in succession the series of despots who had

---

[1] Iamblichus relates this fact in his *Life of Pythagoras*.

brought into subjection Chaldea, Assyria, Persia,
a part of Tartara, Judaea, Syria, and Asia Minor.
Hither Nebuchadnezzar, the assassin of the magi,
had led captive the Jewish people who continued to practise their religion in one corner of the
immense city which would have contained London
four times over. The Jews had even given the
great king a powerful minister in the person of the
prophet Daniel. With Balthazar, the son of Nebuchadnezzar, the walls of the old Babel had finally disappeared beneath the avenging hand of Cyrus, and
Babylon passed for several centuries under Persian
rule. By reason of this series of preceding events,
at the time Pythagoras came there, there were three
different religions side by side in the high priesthood of Babylon : the ancient Chaldean priests, the
survivors of the Persian magi, and the *élite* of the
Jewish captivity. The proof that these different
priesthoods were in mutual agreement, on the esoteric side, is found in the part played by Daniel,
who, whilst acknowledging the God of Moses,
remained first minister under Nebuchadnezzar,
Balthazar, and Cyrus.

Pythagoras was now obliged to enlarge his
horizon, already so vast, by studying these doctrines and religions, the synthesis of which was
still preserved by a few initiates. In Babylon he

was able to thoroughly study the knowledge in the possession of the magi, the heirs of Zoroaster. Though the Egyptian priests alone possessed the universal keys of the sacred sciences, the Persian magi had the reputation of carrying farther the practice of certain arts. They claimed to control those occult powers of nature called pantomorphic fire and astral light. In their temples, it was said, darkness reigned in broad daylight, lamps were lit without human agency, the radiance of the Gods was visible and the rumble of thunder could be heard. The magi gave the name of *celestial lion* to this incorporeal fire, the agent that generates electricity, which they could condense or disperse at will, and that of *serpents* to the electric currents of the atmosphere and the magnetic currents of the earth, which they claimed to be able to direct like arrows against mankind. They had also made a special study of the suggestive, attractive, and creative power of the human word. To evoke spirits they employed graduated formulas, borrowed from the most ancient languages on earth. The following is the psychic reasoning they themselves gave thereof: " Make no change in the barbarous names employed in evocation; for they are the pantheistic names of God; they are magnetized with the worship of multitudes, and their power is

ineffable." [1] These evocations, accompanied by
prayer and purification, were, properly speaking,
what was called at a later date, white magic.

Accordingly we now see Pythagoras in Babylon,
penetrating the arcana of ancient magic. At the
same time, in this den of despotism, he witnessed a
glorious spectacle; on the ruins of the crumbling
religions of the East, above their decimated and
degenerate priesthood, a band of dauntless initiates,
grouped together, were defending their science,
their faith, and as well as they could, justice.
Boldly facing the despots, like Daniel in the den of
lions, ever prepared to be torn to pieces, they
tamed and fascinated the wild beast of absolute
power by their intellectual might, disputing, foot
by foot, the ground they had won.

After his Egyptian and Chaldaean initiation, the
child of Samos knew far more than his teachers of
natural philosophy, far more than any Greek, either
priest or laic, of his time. He was acquainted with
the eternal principles of the universe and their
application. Nature had opened up to him her
secrets; the gross veils of matter had been torn from
his eyes, enabling him to see the marvellous
spheres of nature and spiritualized humanity. In
the temples of Neith-Isis in Memphis, and Bel in

[1] *The Oracles of Zoroaster*, taken from the theurgy of Proclus.

Babylon, he had learned many secrets as to the past history of religions, continents, and races. He had been able to compare the advantages with the disadvantages of the Jewish monotheism, the Greek polytheism, the Hindu trinitarianism, and the Persian dualism. He knew that all these religions were rays of one same truth, strained down through different degrees of intelligence and intended for different social conditions. He held the key, *i. e.* the synthesis of all these doctrines, in esoteric science. His vision, compassing the past and plunging into the future, was bound to judge the present with singular lucidity. His experience showed him humanity threatened with the most terrible evils, through the ignorance of the priests, the materialism of the savants, and the lack of discipline in the democracies. In the midst of this universal decay he saw Asiatic despotism increase; from this dark cloud a terrible cyclone was about to burst upon defenceless Europe.

Accordingly it was now the hour to return to Greece, there to fulfil his mission and begin his work.

Pythagoras had been kept in Babylon for twelve years. To leave the city, an order from the king of Persia was necessary. Democedes, a compatriot of his and the king's physician, interceded in his

favour and obtained liberty for the philosopher.
After an absence of thirty-four years Pythagoras
returned to Samos. He found his country crushed
and ruined by a satrap of the great king. Schools
and temples were closed, poets and savants had fled
like a cloud of swallows before Persian caesarism.
He had the consolation however, of seeing Hermodamas, his first master, take his last breath, and of
meeting Parthenis, his mother, the only one who
had never doubted that he would return. For every-
one thought that the adventurous son of the jeweller
of Samos was dead. Not for a moment had she
doubted the oracle of Apollo. Well she divined
that beneath the Egyptian priest's white robe, her
son was preparing himself for some lofty mission.
She knew that there would come forth from the
temple of Neith-Isis the beneficent master, the light-
bearing prophet, of whom she had dreamed in the
sacred wood of Delphi, and whom the hierophant of
Adonaï had promised her beneath the cedars of
Lebanon.

And now a light skiff was bearing away mother
and son to a new exile over the azure waves of the
Aegean sea. They were fleeing, with all their possessions, from an oppressed and ruined Samos, and
were making sail for Greece. Neither the Olympic
crowns nor the poet's laurels tempted the son of

Parthenis. His work was greater and more mysterious; it was to rouse to life the slumbering soul of the gods in the sanctuaries, to restore the temple of Apollo to its former might and prestige, and then to found somewhere a school of science and of life whence should come forth, not politicians and sophists, but men and women initiates, true mothers and pure heroes!

CHAPTER III

THE TEMPLE OF DELPHI—THE SCIENCE OF
APOLLO—THEORY OF DIVINATION—THE
PYTHONESS THEOCLEA

FROM the plain of Phocis the traveller mounts the
smiling meadows bordering the banks of the
Pleistus to plunge into a winding valley shut in
between lofty mountains. At every step the way
becomes narrower and the country more sublime and
deserted. Finally a circle of rugged mountains,
crowned with wild-looking peaks, a veritable store-
house of electricity, over which storms often raged,
is reached. Suddenly, far up the sombre gorge
appears the town of Delphi, like an eagle's nest, on
a rock surrounded by precipices and dominated by
the two peaks of Parnassus. From the distance the
bronze Victories are seen sparkling in the light, as
well as the brazen horses, the innumerable statues
of gold, marshalled along the sacred path and
arranged like a guard of heroes and gods round the
Doric temple of Phœbus Apollo.

This was the most sacred spot in Greece. Here,

the Pythoness prophesied and the Amphictyons assembled; here, the different Hellenic peoples had built round the sanctuary chapels containing treasured offerings. Here, processions of men, women, and children, coming from afar, mounted the sacred path to greet the God of Light. From time immemorial religion had consecrated Delphi to the veneration of the people. Its central situation in Hellas, its rock sheltered from profane hands and easy to defend, had contributed to this result. The place was calculated to strike the imagination, for a singular quality gave it great prestige. In a cavern behind the temple was a cleft in the rock from which issued a cold, vapoury mist, inducing, it was said, a state of inspiration and ecstasy. Plutarch relates that in by-gone times a shepherd, when seated by the side of this cleft, began to prophesy. At first he was looked upon as mad, but when his predictions became realized, people began to investigate. The priests took possession of the spot and consecrated it to the divinity. Hence the institution of the Pythoness, who was seated above the cleft on a tripod. The vapours exhaling from the abyss occasioned convulsions and strange crises, provoking in her that *second sight* noticed in certain somnambulists. Eschylus, whose affirmation is not without weight, for he was the son of a priest of

3

Eleusis, and an initiate himself, tells us in his *Eumenides*, by the mouth of the Pythoness, that Delphi had first been consecrated to the Earth, then to Themis (Justice), afterwards to Phœbe (the interceding moon), and finally to Apollo, the solar god. In temple symbolism each of these names represents long periods, and embraces centuries of time. The fame of Delphi, however, dates from Apollo. Jupiter, according to the poets, wishing to find the centre of the earth, started two eagles in their flight from east and west, and they met at Delphi. Whence comes this prestige, this world-wide and unchallenged authority which constituted Apollo as the god of Greece *par excellence,* and now makes the glory of his name inexplicable to us?

History is dumb on this important point. Question orators, poets, and philosophers, they will only give you superficial explanations. The real answer to this question remained the secret of the temple. Let us try to fathom it.

In Orphic thought, Dionysos and Apollo were two different revelations of the same divinity. Dionysos represented esoteric truth, the foundation and interior of things, open to initiates alone. He held the mysteries of life, past and future existences, the relations between soul and body, heaven and earth. Apollo personified the same truth applied to

life on earth and social order. The inspirer of
poetry, medicine, and laws, he was science by
divination, beauty by art, peace among nations by
justice, and harmony between soul and body by
purification. In a word, to the initiate Dionysos
signified nothing less than the divine spirit in evolution in the universe; and Apollo, the manifestation
thereof to mankind on earth. The people had been
made to understand this by a legend. The priests
had told them that, in the time of Orpheus,
Bacchus and Apollo had vied with one another for
the tripod of Delphi. Bacchus had willingly given
it up to his brother, and withdrawn to one of the
peaks of Parnassus, where the Theban women were
wont to celebrate his mysteries. In reality the
two sons of Jupiter divided between themselves
the empire of the world. The one reigned
over the mysterious Beyond, the other over the
World of the Living.

So that we find in Apollo the solar Logos, the
universal Word, the mighty Mediator, the Vishnu
of the Hindus, the Mithras of the Persians, and the
Horus of the Egyptians. The old ideas of Asiatic
esoterism, however, took on, in the legend of
Apollo, a plastic beauty, and an incisive splendour
which made them penetrate the more deeply into
human consciousness, like the shafts of the God.

" White-winged serpents springing forth from his golden bow," says Eschylus.

Apollo springs forth from the mighty night at Delos; all the goddesses greet his birth; he walks and takes up his bow and lyre, his locks stream in the air and his quiver rattles on his shoulder; the sea quivers, and the whole island shines with his glory scattered abroad in floods of golden flame. This is the epiphany of divine light, which by its august presence creates order, splendour, and harmony, of which poetry is the marvellous echo. The god goes to Delphi and pierces with his arrows a monstrous serpent which was ravaging and laying waste the land, he purifies the country and establishes the temple; the image of the victory of this divine light over darkness and evil. In ancient religions, the serpent symbolized at once the fatal circle of life and the evil resulting therefrom. And yet, from this life once understood and overcome, springs forth knowledge. Apollo, slayer of the serpent, is the symbol of the initiate who pierces nature by science, tames it by his will, and breaking the Karmic circle of the flesh mounts aloft in spiritual splendour, whilst the broken fragments of human animality lie writhing in the sand. For this reason Apollo is the master of expiation, of the purification of soul and body. Bespattered with

the monster's blood, he performed expiation, purified himself during an eight years' exile beneath the
bitter, health-giving laurels of the vale of Tempe.—
Apollo, trainer of men, likes to take up his abode
in their midst, he is pleased to be in towns with the
youths and young men, at contests of poetry and
the palaestra, though he remains only for a time.
In autumn he returns to his own land, the home of
the Hyperboreans. This is the mysterious people
of luminous and transparent souls who dwell in the
eternal dawn of perfect felicity. Here are his true
priests, his beloved priestesses. He lives with them
in strong, intimate communion, and when he wishes
to make mankind a royal gift, he brings back from
the country of the Hyperboreans one of those
mighty, radiant souls who is born on earth to teach
and delight mortals. He himself returns to Delphi
every spring, when poems and hymns are sung in
his honour. Visible to none but initiates he comes
in dazzling Hyperborean glory, in a chariot drawn
by sweetly-singing swans. Again he takes up his
abode in the sanctuary, where the Pythoness speaks
forth his oracles, and sages and poets listen. Then
is heard the song of nightingales, the fountain of
Castalia scatters silver spray on every hand,
dazzling light and celestial music penetrate the
heart of man and reach the very veins of nature.

In this legend of the Hyperboreans may be found much light thrown on the esoteric basis of the Apollo myth. The land of the Hyperboreans is the Beyond, the empyrean of victorious souls, whose astral dawns light up its many-coloured zones. Apollo himself personifies the immaterial and intelligible light of which the sun is merely the physical image, and from which flows down all truth. The wonderful swans which bring him are poets and divine geniuses, messengers of his mighty solar soul, leaving behind them flashes of light and strains of glorious music. Hyperborean Apollo, accordingly, personifies the descent of heaven on to earth, the incarnation of spiritual beauty in flesh and blood, the inflow of transcendent truth by inspiration and divination.

It is now the moment to raise the golden veil of legend and enter the temple itself. How was divination practised therein? Here we touch upon the secrets of Apollonian science and of the mysteries of Delphi.

In antiquity, a strong tie united divination to the solar cults, and here we have the golden key to all the so-called magic mysteries.

The worship of Aryan humanity from the beginning of civilization was directed towards the sun as the source of light, heat, and life. When, how-

ever, the thought of the sages rose from the phenomenon to the cause, behind this sensible fire, this
visible light, they formed the concept of an immaterial fire, an intelligible light. They identified
the form with the male principle, the creative spirit
or intellectual essence of the universe, and the latter
with its female principle, its formative soul, its
plastic substance. This intuition dates back to time
immemorial. The conception I speak of is connected with the most ancient mythologies. It circulates in the Vedic hymns under the form of Agni,
the universal fire which penetrates all things. It
blossoms forth in the religion of Zoroaster, the esoteric part of which is represented by the cult of
Mithras. Mithras is the male fire and Mitra the
female light. Zoroaster formally states that the
Eternal, by means of the living Word, created the
heavenly light, the seed of Ormuzd, the principle of
material light and material fire. For the initiate of
Mithras the sun is only a rude reflection of this
light. In his obscure grotto, whose vault is painted
with stars, he invokes the sun of grace, the fire of
love, conqueror of evil, reconciler of Ormuzd and
Ahriman, purifier and mediator, who dwells in the
soul of the holy prophets. In the crypts of Egypt,
the initiates seek this same sun under the name of
Osiris. When Hermes asks to be allowed to con-

template the origin of things, at first he feels himself plunged into the ethereal waves of a delicious light, in which move all living forms. Then, plunging into the darkness of dense matter, he hears a voice which he recognizes as *the voice of light*. At the same time fire darts forth from the depths, immediately all is light and chaos becomes order. In the *Book of the Dead* of the Egyptians the souls journey painfully towards that light in the barque of Isis. Moses fully adopted this doctrine in Genesis: '' Elohim said: Let there be light; and there was light.'' Now the creation of this light precedes that of the sun and stars. This means that, in the order of principles and cosmogony, intelligible precedes material light. The Greeks, who moulded into human form and dramatized the most abstract ideas, expressed the same doctrine in the myth of Hyperborean Apollo.

Consequently the human mind, by inner contemplation of the universe, from the point of view of the soul and the intelligence, came to conceive of an intelligible light, an imponderable element serving as an intermediary between matter and spirit. It would be easy to show that natural philosophers of modern times insensibly draw somewhere near the same conclusion along an opposite path, *i. e.* by searching for the constitution of matter and seeing

the impossibility of explaining it by itself. Even in
the sixteenth century, Paracelsus, whilst studying
the chemical combinations and metamorphoses of
bodies, went so far as to admit of a universal occult
agent by means of which they are brought about.
The natural philosophers of the sixteenth and seven-
teenth centuries, who conceived of the universe as
being a dead machine, believed in the absolute void
of celestial space. Yet when it was discovered that
light is not the emission of a radiant matter, but
rather the vibration of an imponderable element,
one was obliged to admit that the whole of space is
filled by an infinitely subtile fluid penetrating all
bodies and through which waves of heat and light
are transmitted. Thus a return was made to the
Greek ideas of natural philosophy and theosophy.
Newton, who had spent his whole life in studying
the movements of the heavenly bodies, went even
farther than this. He called this ether *sensorium
Dei,* or the brain of God, *i. e.* the organ by which
divine thought acts in the infinitely great as well
as in the infinitely small. In emitting this idea,
which he regarded as necessary to explain the
simple rotation of the heavenly bodies, the great
natural philosopher had embarked on the open
sea of esoteric philosophy. The very ether Newton's thought found in space Paracelsus had dis-

covered at the bottom of his alembics, and had named it astral light. Now this imponderable fluid, which is everywhere present, penetrating all things, this subtile but indispensable agent, this light, invisible to our eyes, but which is at the bottom of all phosphorescence and scintillation, has been proved to exist by a German natural philosopher in a series of well-appointed experiments. Reichenbach had noticed that subjects of very sensitive nerve fibre, when placed in a perfectly dark room in front of a magnet, saw at its two ends strong rays of red, yellow, and blue light. Sometimes these rays vibrated with an undulatory movement. He continued his experiments with all kinds of bodies, especially with crystals. Luminous emanations were seen, by sensitive subjects, round all these bodies. Around the heads of men placed in the dark room they saw white rays; from their fingers issued small flames. In the first portion of their sleep somnambulists sometimes see their magnetizer with these same signs. Pure astral light appears only in a condition of lofty ecstasy, but it is polarized in all bodies, combines with all terrestrial fluids and plays diverse *rôles* in electricity, in terrestrial and animal magnetism.[1] The

[1] Reichenbach called this fluid *odyle*. His work has been translated into English by Gregory: *Researches on Magnetism, Electricity, Heat, Light, Cristalization and Chemical Attraction.*—London, 1850.

interest of Reichenbach's experiments is that they make precise the limits and transition from physical to astral vision capable of leading on to spiritual vision. They also enable us to obtain a faint glimpse of the infinite subtilties of imponderable matter. Along this path there is nothing to prevent our conceiving it as so fluid, so subtile and penetrating, that it becomes in some way homogeneous with spirit, serving the latter as a perfect garment.

We have just seen that modern natural philosophy, in order to explain the world, has been obliged to recognize an imponderable, universal agent, that it has even proved its presence, and, in this way, without knowing it, has fallen in with the notions of ancient theosophies. Let us now try to define the nature and function of cosmic fluid in accordance with the philosophy of occultism in all ages. On this main principle of cosmogony, Zoroaster is in agreement with Heraclitus, Pythagoras with Saint Paul, the Kabbalists with Paracelsus. Cybele-Maïa reigns everywhere, the mighty soul of the world, the vibrating and plastic substance which the breath of the creative spirit uses at its will. Her oceans of ether serve to cement together all the worlds. She is the great mediator between the invisible and the visible, between spirit and matter,

between the within and the without of the universe.
Condensed in enormous masses in the atmosphere
beneath the action of the sun, she flashes forth in a
thunderbolt.   Absorbed by the earth she circulates
in magnetic currents.   Subtilized in the nervous
system of the animal she transmits her will to the
limbs, her sensations to the brain.   More than that,
this subtile fluid forms living organisms similar to
material bodies.   It serves as substance to the astral
body of the soul, a garment of light which the spirit
is ever weaving for itself.   The fluid becomes transformed, it rarefies or densifies according to the souls
it clothes or the worlds it envelops.   Not only does
it embody spirit and spiritualize matter in its living
bosom, it reflects in a perpetual mirage both things
and the thoughts and wills of mankind.   The
strength and duration of these images is in proportion to the intensity of the will producing them.
And, in truth, there is no other means of explaining
thought suggestion and transmission at a distance,
that principle of magic now-a-days acknowledged
and recognized by science.[1]   Thus in the astral
light the past of the worlds trembles in vague
images, and the future is there also, with the living

[1] See the Bulletin of the Société de Pyschologie Physiologique.   M.
Charcot, president, 1885.   See more especially the fine book by M.
Ochorowicz, *De la Suggestion Mentale*, Paris, 1887.

souls inevitably destined to descend into flesh. This is the meaning of the veil of Isis and the mantle of Cybele, into which all beings are woven.

It is now seen that the theosophical doctrine of the astral light is identical with the secret doctrine of the solar Word in the religions of Greece and the East. It is also seen how closely allied this doctrine is to that of divination. The astral light is there revealed as the universal medium of the phenomena of vision and of ecstasy which it explains. It is at once the vehicle which transmits the movements of thought, and the living mirror in which the soul contemplates the images of the material and spiritual world. Once transported into this element, the spirit of the seer leaves corporeal conditions. For him the measure of time and space is changed. In some way he participates in the ubiquity of the universal fluid. For him opaque matter becomes transparent, and the soul, disengaging itself from the body and rising in its own light, penetrates, in a state of ecstasy, into the spiritual world, sees souls clothed in their ethereal bodies and communicates with them. All the initiates of former times had a clear notion of this *second sight*, or direct spiritual vision. Witness Eschylus, who puts into the mouth of the shade of Clytemnestra :

" Look at these wounds, thy spirit can see them; when one is asleep, the spirit possesses a more piercing vision; in broad daylight, the eyes of mortals see but a little way."

Let me add that this theory of clairvoyance and ecstasy is in wonderful agreement with the numerous experiments, scientifically carried out by savants and doctors of modern times, on lucid somnambulists and clairvoyants of every kind.[1] From these contemporary facts I shall endeavour briefly to characterize the successive psychic conditions from simple clairvoyance to cataleptic ecstasy.

The state of clairvoyance, as is seen by thousands

[1] There is a great deal of literature on this subject, very unequal in value, in France, Germany and England. I will here mention two books in which the subject is treated scientifically by men of real worth.

(1) *Letters on Animal Magnetism*, by William Gregory, London, 1850. Gregory was a professor of chemistry at the University of Edinburgh. His book is a profound study of the phenomena of animal magnetism, from suggestion to vision at a distance and lucid clairvoyance, on subjects observed by himself, in accordance with scientific method, and with minute exactness.

(2) *Die mystischen Erscheinungen der menschlichen Natur*, von Maximilian Perty, Leipzig, 1872. Perty is a professor of philosophy and medicine at the University of Berne. His book presents an immense repertory of all such occult phenomena as have historical value. The extremely remarkable chapter on clairvoyance (Schlafwachen), Volume I., contains twenty accounts of female and five of male clairvoyants, related by the doctors who treated the cases. That of Weiner, treated by the author, is most curious. See also the treatises on magnetism by Dupotet and Deleuze, and the very strange book, *Die Seherin von Prévorst*, by Justinus Kerner.

of well-established facts, is a psychic one, differing as greatly from sleep as from a waking condition. The intellectual faculties of the clairvoyant, far from diminishing, increase in marvellous fashion. His memory is more correct, his imagination more active, his intelligence more alert. The main point, in a word, is that we have here developed a new sense, which is no longer corporeal, but rather belongs to the soul. Not only are the thoughts of the magnetizer transmitted to him as in the simple phenomenon of suggestion, which itself is outside the physical plane, but the clairvoyant even reads the thoughts of those present, sees through walls, penetrates hundreds of miles into homes where he has never been, and reads the private life of people he does not know. His eyes are closed, incapable of seeing anything, but his spirit sees farther and better than his open eyes and seems to travel about freely in space.[1] In a word, though clairvoyance may be abnormal from the bodily point of view, it is a normal and superior state from the point of view of the spirit. The consciousness has become deeper, the vision wider. The ego remains the same, but it has passed over to a higher plane, where the vision, freed from the coarse organs of the body, embraces

[1] Numerous examples in Gregory's work: Letters XVI, XVII, and XVIII.

and penetrates a vaster horizon.[1]   It is to be noted
that certain somnambulists, when submitting to the
passes of the magnetizer, feel themselves flooded
with increasingly dazzling light, whilst the awaking
seems to them an unpleasant return to darkness.

[1] The German philosopher, Schelling, has acknowledged the great
importance of somnambulism in the question of the immortality of the
soul.   He remarks that, in lucid sleep, there is produced an elevation
of the soul, and its relative liberation with regard to the body, which
does not take place in the normal state.   In somnambulists, everything
indicates the loftiest consciousness, as though their whole being were
met in one luminous focus, uniting together, past, present and future.
Far from losing all memory of the past, it lies open before them, and
even the veil of the future is at times cast aside in a glorious ray of
light.   If this is possible in earthly life, Schelling inquires, is it not
certain that our spiritual personality, which follows us in death, is at
this very moment present in us, that it is not born then but simply set
free, and shows itself when it is no longer bound by the senses to the
outside world?   The post-mortem condition is accordingly more real
than the earthly one.   For in this life, that which is accidental, mingling with the whole, paralyzes in us that which is essential.   Schelling
calls the future state quite simply, clairvoyance.   The spirit liberated
from everything accidental in earthly life becomes stronger and more
alive ; the wicked man becomes worse, the good better.

Quite recently Charles du Prel has advanced the same opinion,
supporting it with numerous facts and details in a well-written volume,
Philosophie der Mystik (1886).   He starts from this fact : the consciousness of the ego does not exhaust its object.   " Soul and consciousness are not two adequate terms ; they do not cover one another as
they have not an equal scope.   The sphere of the soul far surpasses
that of the consciousness."   Consequently there is *a latent ego* in us.
This latent ego, which manifests itself in sleep and in dreams, is the real
ego, supra-terrestrial and transcendent, whose existence precedes our
terrestrial ego which is bound to the body.   The terrestrial ego is
perishable, the transcendent ego is immortal.   This is what St. Pau
meant when he said—"——the Lord Jesus Christ, who shall change
our vile body, so that it be fashioned like unto His glorious body."

Suggestion, thought reading, and distant vision are facts which already prove the independent existence of the soul, and transport us above the physical plane of the universe without making us leave it altogether. Clairvoyance, however, has infinite varieties and a scale of different states far wider than that of the waking condition. In proportion as the scale is mounted the phenomena become rarer and more extraordinary. I will mention only the principal stages. *Retrospection* is a vision of past events preserved in the astral light and revived by the sympathy of the seer. *Divination,* properly so called, is a problematical vision of things to come either by introspection of the thoughts of the living which contain future actions in germ, or by the occult influence of superior spirits which unfold the future in living images before the soul of the clairvoyant. In both cases they are projections of thoughts into the astral light. Finally *ecstasy* is defined as a vision of the spiritual world, where good or evil spirits appear to the seer in human form and communicate with him. The soul seems really to be transported out of the body, which life has almost left, and which stiffens into a state of catalepsy resembling death. From what those who have been in a condition of sublime ecstasy tell us, nothing in the universe can express

4

the beauty and splendour of these visions, or the sentiment of an ineffable fusion with the divine essence which they bring back, a very transport of light and music.   The reality of these visions may be doubted.   It must, nevertheless, be added that if the soul, in the average state of clairvoyance, has a correct perception of distant places and of absent ones, it is logical to admit that, in its loftiest exalta-tion, it may have the vision of a higher and an immaterial reality.

In my opinion, it will be the task of the future to restore to the transcendent faculties of the human soul their dignity and social function, by reorganiz-ing them under the control of science and on the basis of a religion which is truly universal, open to all truths.   Then science, regenerated by real faith and the spirit of love, will, with open eyes, mount aloft to those spheres in which speculative philo-sophy gropes about with bandaged eyes.   Yes, science will become clear-sighted and redeeming in her mission, just in proportion as the consciousness and love of humanity increase in her.   Perhaps it is through " the gate of sleep and dreams," as Homer said, that divine Psyche, banished from our civilized life and weeping in silence beneath her veil, will regain possession of her altars.

Anyhow, the phenomena of clairvoyance, studied

from every aspect by present-day savants and doctors, throw an altogether new light on the *rôle* of divination in antiquity and on a host of apparently supernatural phenomena, with which the annals of every nation and people are filled. Of course, a distinction must be made between legend and history, hallucination and real vision. Still, the experimental psychology of our times teaches us not to reject, in a body, facts which fall within human possibility, but rather to investigate them from the point of view of well-ascertained laws. If clairvoyance is a faculty of the soul, we may no longer simply consign prophets, oracles, and sybils to the domain of superstition. Divination has really been known and practised in temples of old, with fixed principles and a social and religious end in view. The comparative study of religions and esoteric traditions shows that these principles were the same everywhere, although their application may have varied infinitely. What has discredited the art of divination is that its corruption has given rise to the worst abuses, and that its glorious manifestations are possible only in beings of exceptional purity.

Divination, as practised at Delphi, was founded on the principles we have just set forth, the inner organization of the temple corresponded thereto.

As in the great temples of Egypt, it consisted of an art and a science. The art consisted in penetrating the far-away past and future by clairvoyance or prophetic ecstasy; the science, in calculating the future in accordance with the laws of universal evolution. Art and science checked one another. All I will say of this science, called genethlialogy by the ancients, and of which the astrology of the middle ages is only an imperfectly understood fragment, is that it took for granted the esoteric encyclopedia as applied to the future of peoples and individuals. Though very useful in showing the direction things were taking, it was always of very doubtful application. Only the very loftiest minds knew how to use it. Pythagoras had thoroughly mastered it in Egypt, but in Greece it was practised with a less thorough or clear understanding. On the other hand, clairvoyance and prophecy had made considerable progress.

It is well known that this art was practised in Delphi through the agency of women, both young and old. They were called Pythonesses, and played the passive *rôle* of clairvoyant somnambulists. Their oracles, often obscure, were interpreted, translated, and arranged by the priests in accordance with their own lights. Modern historians have seen in the institution of Delphi scarcely anything more than the exploitation of superstition by intelligent charlatans. Besides the assent, however, given by the whole of philosophic antiquity to the Delphic science of divination, several oracles related by Herodotus, such as those regarding Croesus and the battle of Salamis, speak in its favour. Doubtless their art had its beginning, its condition of prosperity, and its decay. Charlatanism and corruption exercised their demoralizing influence in the end, as we see in the case of king Cleomenes, who bribed the high priestess of Delphi to deprive Demaratus of his throne. Plutarch wrote a treatise inquiring into the reasons for the decline and extinction of the oracles; this degeneracy was felt to be a misfortune throughout all classes of antiquity. At first, divination was practised with a degree of religious sincerity and scientific thoroughness which raised it to the height of a real ministration. On the pediment of the temple could be read the inscription: " Know thyself," and another one above the entrance door: " Let no one enter here with impure hands." These words explained to all comers that earthly passions, falsehood and hypocrisy were not to pass the threshold of the sanctuary, that within, in awe-inspiring solemnity, reigned divine Truth.

Pythagoras reached Delphi only after having

visited all the temples of Greece. He had stayed with Epimenides in the sanctuary of Idaean Jupiter; he had been present at the Olympic games, and presided over the mysteries of Eleusis, where the hierophant had given up his place to him. Everywhere had he been received as a master, and now he was expected at Delphi. Here the art of divination was in a languishing condition, and Pythagoras wished to restore its former prestige and might. Accordingly he went there not so much to consult Apollo as to enlighten his interpreters and revive their enthusiasm and energy. Through them his influence would mould the soul of Greece and prepare a future for the land.

Fortunately he found in the temple a marvellous instrument reserved for him, to all appearance, by the hand of Providence.

Young Theoclea belonged to the college of the priestesses of Apollo. She sprang from one of those families in which the priestly dignity is hereditary. Her childhood had been fed on the mighty impressions imparted by the sanctuary, the ceremonies, pæans, and *fêtes* of Pythian and Hyperborean Apollo. Evidently she was one of those maidens born with an instinctive abhorrence for the things which attracted others. They love not Ceres and fear Venus, for the heavy atmosphere of earth troubles them, and the vague glimpse they have obtained of physical love seems to them the rape of the soul, the pollution of their undefiled, virginal being. On the other hand, they are strangely sensitive to mysterious currents, to astral influences. When the moon was shedding her soft beams on the sombre groves near the fountain of Castalia, Theoclea would see white forms gliding by. She heard voices in open daylight. On exposing herself to the rays of the rising sun, their vibration threw her into a kind of ecstasy, during which she heard the singing of invisible choirs. At the same time she was quite indifferent to popular superstition and idolatry; a feeling of horror overcame her at the sacrifices of animals. She spoke to no one regarding the apparitions which disturbed her sleep, feeling with clairvoyant instinct that the priests of Apollo were not in possession of that supreme light she needed. The latter, however, had fixed on her with the object of persuading her to become Pythoness. She felt herself attracted by a higher world to which she had not the key. What were these gods who manifested themselves to her in vibrations which troubled her being, and to whom she owed her inspiration? This she would know before giving herself up to them, for great souls need to see clearly even in abandoning themselves to divine powers.

With what a deep thrill, with how mysterious a presentiment the soul of Theoclea must have been stirred when she saw Pythagoras for the first time, and heard his eloquent voice resound among the columns of the sanctuary of Apollo! She felt the presence of the initiator for whom she was waiting, she recognized her master. She wished to know; knowledge would come by him; he would make this inner world speak, this world she bore within herself!—He, on his side, must have recognized in her, with sure and penetrating glance, the living, thrilling soul he was seeking, to become the interpreter of his thoughts in the temple and instil therein a new spirit. No sooner had their eyes met, their lips spoken, than an invisible chain bound the sage of Samos to the young priestess, who listened to him without a word, drinking in his utterances with eager, attentive eyes. Some one has said that a profound vibration enables poet and lyre to recognize one another as they approach. Thus did Pythagoras and Theoclea recognize one another.

At sunrise, Pythagoras had long conversations with the priests of Apollo, ordained saints and prophets. He requested that the young priestess should be received by them, so that he might initiate her into his secret teaching and prepare her for her mission. Accordingly she was permitted to follow the lessons given daily in the sanctuary by the master. Pythagoras was now in the prime of life. He wore a white robe, girdled in Egyptian fashion; a purple band was wrapped round his majestic brow. When he spoke, his grave, mild eyes were fastened on his interlocutor, enveloping him in a warm, tender light. The very atmosphere seemed to become lighter and electric with intelligence.

The conversations of the sage of Samos with the highest representatives of the Greek religion were of the utmost importance. It was not merely a question of divination and inspiration, the future of Greece and the destiny of the whole world were at stake. The knowledge, titles, and powers he had acquired in the temples of Memphis and Babylon gave him the greatest authority and influence. To those who inspired Greece he had the right to speak as a superior and a guide. This he did with all the eloquence of his genius and the enthusiasm of his mission. To enlighten their minds, he began by telling them of his youthful days, his struggles and Egyptian initiation. He spoke to them of Egypt, the mother of Greece, old as the world itself, immovable as a mummy, covered with hieroglyphs in the recesses of its pyramids, though possessing in its tombs the secrets of peoples, languages, and religions. Before their eyes he unfolded the mysteries of great Isis, goddess of earth and heaven,

mother of gods and men; then, relating his trials
and ordeals, he plunged them, with himself, into
the light of Osiris. Afterwards came the turn of
Babylon, of the Chaldaean magi, their occult
sciences, and those deep solid temples where they
call forth the living fire, the abode of demons and
gods.

As she listened to Pythagoras, Theoclea passed
through wonderful sensations. All he said was
branded in letters of fire in her mind. These things
appeared to her both marvellous and yet well
known. Instead of hearing something new she
seemed to be recalling what she had already
learned. The master's words set her turning over
the pages of the universe like those of a book. No
longer did she see the gods in their human image,
but in their essence, forming things and spirits.
With them she flowed in space, rising and falling.
At times there came the illusion that she no longer
felt the limits of her body, and was fading away
into infinity. Thus her imagination entered by
degrees into the invisible world, and the former
traces she found of it in her own soul told her that
this was the true and only reality; the other was
only apparent. She felt that her inner eyes would
soon open and read the truth.

From these heights the master suddenly brought
her back to earth by relating the misfortunes of

Egypt. After developing the greatness of Egyptian science, he showed how it was dying away under the Persian invasion. He depicted the horrible atrocities committed by Cambyses, the pillaged temples, the sacred books committed to the flames, the priests of Osiris killed or dispersed, the monster of Persian despotism collecting beneath his iron hand all the old barbaric tribes of Asia, the half-savage nomad races of India, and the centre of the continent, awaiting only a favourable opportunity to fall upon Europe. Yes, this ever-increasing cyclone must burst upon Greece as certainly as the thunderbolt, collecting in the sky, must flash forth from the cloud. Was divided Greece prepared to resist this terrible attack? She did not even suspect it. Nations cannot avoid their destinies, which the gods precipitate upon them, unless they are ever watchful. Had not Egypt, that wise nation of Hermes, crumbled to ruin after six thousand years of prosperity? Greece, alas! and beautiful Ionia will pass away even sooner! A time will come when the solar god will abandon this temple, when barbarian tribes will overthrow its very walls, and shepherds lead their flocks to pasture on the ruins of Delphi.

Before such sinister prophecies the countenance of Theoclea became transformed, assuming a terrified expression. She sank to the ground, and, with arms clasped round a column and eyes fixed as though plunged in thought, she resembled the genius of Grief weeping over the tomb of Greece.

"Those are secrets," continued Pythagoras, "which must be buried in the depths of the temples. The initiate attracts death or repels it at his pleasure. By forming the magic chain of wills, initiates in this way prolong the life of nations. It is for you to postpone the fatal hour, to cause Greece to shine in splendour and beam forth with the word of Apollo. Nations and peoples are what their gods make them, but the gods reveal themselves only to such as appeal to them. What is Apollo? The word of the one God manifesting himself eternally in the world. Truth is the soul of God, his body is the light. Only seers, sages, and prophets behold it; men see only its shadow. Legions of glorified spirits, whom we call heroes and demi-gods, inhabit this light in spheres beyond number. This is the real body of Apollo, the sun of initiates, without his rays nothing great is done on earth. As the magnet attracts iron, so by our thoughts, our prayers, and actions do we attract divine inspiration. It is for you to hand over to Greece the word of Apollo, and Greece shall be resplendent with immortal light!"

With such language Pythagoras succeeded in restoring to the priests of Delphi the consciousness of their mission. Theoclea drank in every word with silent, concentrated passion. She was visibly becoming transformed beneath the thought and will of the master as by a slow incantation. Standing in the midst of the astonished elders, she untied her raven-black locks and thrust them back from her head as though she felt flames of fire playing in and about them. Her eyes, transfigured and wide open, seemed to behold the solar and planetary gods in their radiant, glowing orbs.

One day she fell into a deep, lucid sleep. The five prophets surrounded her, but she remained insensible alike to their voice and touch. Pythagoras drew near and said: " Rise and go where my thought sends thee. For now thou art the Pythoness !"

On hearing the master's voice, a long vibrating thrill ran through the whole of her body and she rose to her feet. Her eyes were closed, but she saw from within.

" Where art thou ?" asked Pythagoras.

" I am ascending——ascending all the time."

" And now ?"

" I am bathing in the light of Orpheus."

" What seest thou in the future ?"

"Great wars——men of might—— Apollo returns to dwell in his sanctuary, and I shall be his voice——! But thou, his messenger, thou art about to leave me, alas! thou wilt bear the torch of his light into Italy."

Long did the seer speak, with closed eyes, in musical, panting, rhythmic voice; then suddenly, with a sob, she fell to the ground like one dead.

Thus did Pythagoras pour a pure, undefiled stream of knowledge into Theoclea's breast, tuning her like a lyre for divine inspiration. Once exalted to these heights she became his torch, thanks to which he was able to sound his own destiny, see into the possible future, and direct his path along the strandless zones of the invisible. Such a striking counter-verification of the truths he taught filled the priests with admiration, aroused their courage and revived their faith. The temple now possessed an inspired Pythoness, and priests initiated into the divine sciences and arts; Delphi could once again become a centre of life and action.

Pythagoras remained there for a whole year. It was only after imparting to the priests all the secrets of his doctrine, and preparing Theoclea for his ministry, that he took his departure for Greater Greece.

CHAPTER IV

THE ORDER AND THE DOCTRINE

THE town of Croton was situated at the extremity
of the Gulf of Tarentum, near the Lacinian promontory, in front of the open sea. Like Sybaris, it was
one of the most flourishing cities in Southern Italy.
It was famed for its Doric constitution, its victorious athletes at the Olympian games, and its
doctors, rivals of the Asclepiads. The Sybarites
owe their immortality to their luxury and effemin-
acy. The inhabitants of Croton would perhaps be
forgotten, spite of their virtues, had theirs not been
the glory of offering a home to the great school of
esoteric philosophy, known under the name of the
Pythagorean sect, which may be looked upon as the
mother of the school of Plato and the ancestor of all
idealist schools. However noble the descendants,
their ancestors greatly surpassed them. The school
of Plato issues from an incomplete tradition,
whereas the Stoic school has already lost the true
tradition. Other systems of ancient and modern
philosophy are more or less fortunate speculations,

whilst the teaching of Pythagoras was based on experimental science and accompanied by a complete organization of life.

The secrets of the master's order and thought are now, like the ruins of the ancient town, buried deep underground. All the same we will try to resurrect them, for thus we shall have an opportunity of penetrating to the very heart of the theosophic doctrine, the arcanum of religions and philosophies, and raising a corner of the veil of Isis to the light of Greek genius.

Several reasons influenced Pythagoras in choosing this Dorian colony as a centre of action. His aim was not merely to teach the esoteric doctrine to a circle of chosen disciples, but also to apply its principles to the education of youth and to the life of the state. This plan comprised the foundation of an institution for laic initiation, with the object of finally transforming the political organization of the cities by degrees into the image of that philosophic and religious ideal. Certainly none of the republics of Hellas or of Peloponnesus would have tolerated this innovation. The philosopher would have been accused of conspiring against the State. The Greek towns of the Gulf of Tarentum, which were less preyed upon by demagogues, were more liberal-minded. Pythagoras made no mistake in expecting to find a favourable reception for his reforms at the hands of the Croton senate. His designs went also beyond Greece. Foreseeing the evolution of ideas, he was prepared for the fall of Hellenism, and was thinking of sowing in the human mind the principles of a scientific religion. By founding his school in the Gulf of Tarentum, he was spreading esoteric ideas throughout Italy, and keeping in the precious vase of his doctrine the purified essence of Oriental wisdom for the peoples of the West.

On coming to Croton, which was at the time inclined to adopt the voluptuous life of its neighbour Sybaris, Pythagoras produced a veritable revolution. Porphyry and Iamblichus have depicted the commencement of his life there as being rather that of a magician than of a philosopher. Assembling the youth in the Temple of Apollo, he succeeded by his eloquence in tearing them away from a life of debauchery. Summoning the women to the Temple of Juno, he persuaded them to bring their golden robes and ornaments as trophies to celebrate the defeat of vanity and luxury. He threw a veil of grace over the austerity of his teachings, a communicating flame flashed forth from his words of wisdom. His beautiful face and noble bearing, the charm of his countenance and of his voice com-

5

pletely captivated them. The women compared him to Jupiter, the young men to Hyperborean Apollo. He captivated and seduced the crowds which, whilst listening to him, were greatly astonished to find themselves enamoured of truth and virtue.

The senate of Croton, or *the Council of the Thousand,* grew uneasy at the influence he was obtaining. They summoned Pythagoras to explain his conduct, and to state the means he was making use of to master the minds of the citizens. This gave him an opportunity to develop his ideas on education, and demonstrate that, far from threatening with ruin the Doric constitution of Croton, they only strengthened it the more. When he had won over to his side the wealthiest of the citizens and the majority of the senate, he proposed that they should found an institute for himself and his disciples. This brotherhood of laic initiates should live in common in a building constructed for the purpose, though without separating themselves from civil life. Those of them who already deserved the name of master, might teach physical, psychic, and religious sciences. Young men should be admitted to the lessons of the masters and to the different grades of initiation according to their intelligence or earnestness in study, under the control of the head of the order. At the beginning, they must submit to the rules of the common life and spend the whole day in the institute, under the supervision of the masters. Those who should wish to enter the order formally were to give up their fortune to a trustee, with permission to enter again into possession of it whenever they pleased. In the institute there would be a section for women, along with a parallel initiation, though different and more adapted to the duties of their sex.

This plan was enthusiastically adopted by the senate of Croton, and, after a few years, near the entrance to the town there rose a building surrounded by vast porticoes and beautiful gardens. The inhabitants of Croton called it the Temple of the Muses, and, to tell the truth, in the centre of the buildings, near the humble dwelling of the master, stood a temple dedicated to these divinities.

Thus sprang into being the Pythagorean institute, which became at one and the same time a college of education, a science academy, and a small model city under the control of a great initiate. It is by theory and practice, by science and art combined that slow progress was made to that science of sciences, that magical harmony of soul and intellect with the universe which Pythagoreans looked upon as the arcanum of philosophy

and religion. The Pythagorean school is of
supreme interest for us, inasmuch as it was a most
remarkable attempt at laic initiation. Being an
anticipated synthesis of Hellenism and Christianity, it grafted the fruit of science on the tree of
life, it acquired the knowledge of that inner, that
living realization, of truth, which a profound faith
alone can give. It was an ephemeral realization,
though one of the greatest importance, instinct with
the fruitfulness of example.

To form some idea of it, let us enter the Pythagorean institute along with the novice and follow
his initiation step by step.

THE TEST

The white dwelling of the brother initiates was
situated on a hill, surrounded by olive and cypress
trees. On mounting from below, the porticoes,
gardens, and gymnasium could distinctly be seen.
The Temple of the Muses, with its circular colonnade
of airy elegance, towered above the two wings of
the building. The terrace of the outer gardens
overlooked the town with its Prytaneum, its harbour
and meeting-place. Away in the distance stretched
the gulf, between sharp rugged parts of the coast

as though in a cup of agate, whilst the Ionian sea shut in the horizon with its line of azure blue. At times one might see women clad in divers-coloured costumes issue on the left and make their way in long files down to the sea, along the alley of cypresses. They were going to worship at the Temple of Ceres. And on the right also, men might often be seen mounting in white robes to the Temple of Apollo. It was not the least attraction to the inquiring imagination of youth to think that the school of the initiates was placed under the protection of these two divinities, one of whom, the Mighty Goddess, held the profound mysteries of Woman and of Earth, whilst the other, the Solar God, revealed those of Man and of Heaven.

So we find this little city of the elect smiling down upon the populous town beneath. The noble instincts of youth were attracted by its peaceful serenity, though nothing was seen of what was taking place within, and it was generally known that admittance was not easily obtained. The gardens connected with the institute of Pythagoras were separated from the outside by nothing but a simple green hedge, and the entrance gate remained open all day long. A statue of Hermes, however, might be seen there, and on its pedestal were the words: *Eskato Bebeloi;* No entrance for the profane! This commandment of the mysteries was universally respected.

Pythagoras was very stern in admitting novices, saying, "that not every kind of wood was fit for making a Mercury." The young men who wished to enter the association were obliged to undergo a period of test and trial. On being introduced by their parents or by one of the masters, they were first of all permitted to enter the Pythagorean gymnasium in which the novices played the games appropriate to their age. The young man at once noticed that this gymnasium was unlike that in the town. There were no violent cries or noisy groups, no ridiculous boasting or vain display of strength by athletes in embryo, challenging one another and exhibiting their muscles; but rather groups of courteous and distinguished-looking young men, walking in couples beneath the porticoes or playing in the arena. They invited him with graceful simplicity to join in their conversation as though he were one of them, without greeting him with a suspicious glance or jeering smile. In the arena they were racing, throwing quoits and javelins, and engaging in mock fights under the form of Doric dances. Pythagoras had, however, strictly abolished wrestling, saying that it was superfluous and even dangerous to develop pride and hatred by strength and agility; that men intended to practise the virtues of friendship ought not to begin by flinging one another on the ground and rolling in the sand like wild beasts; that a real hero could fight with great courage though without fury; that hatred makes us inferior to any opponent whoever he be. The new-comer heard these maxims from the lips of the masters repeated by the novices, who were quite proud to impart their precocious wisdom. At the same time they encouraged him to state his own opinions and freely contradict them. Emboldened by such advances, the ingenuous aspirant quickly showed forth his real nature. Pleased at being listened to and admired, he would speak and dilate at his ease. Meanwhile the masters closely watched him without ever uttering the slightest word of reprimand. Pythagoras would come up unexpectedly and study his gestures and words. He paid special attention to the gait and the laugh of young men. Laughter, he said, is an infallible index to character, no amount of dissimulation can render agreeable the laugh of an evil-disposed man. He had also made such a profound study of the human face that he could read therein the very depths of the soul.[1]

Such minute observation enabled the master to

[1] Origen states that Pythagoras was the inventor of physiognomy.

form a precise idea regarding his future disciples. A few months afterwards came decisive tests in imitation of Egyptian initiation, though greatly modified and adapted to the Greek nature, whose sensitiveness had not submitted to the mortal terrors of the crypts of Memphis and Thebes. The Pythagorean aspirant was made to spend the night in a cavern, in the outskirts of the town, alleged to be haunted by various apparitions and monsters. Those who had not sufficient strength to endure the terrible impressions of solitude and night, who refused to enter or made their escape before the morning, were deemed too weak for initiation and rejected.

The moral test was a more serious one. Suddenly, without the least preparation, the would-be disciple would one fine morning find himself imprisoned in an empty, dismal-looking cell. A slate was given him and he was coldly ordered to discover the meaning of one of the Pythagorean symbols, as, for instance : What is the signification of the triangle inscribed in a circle ? or : Why is the dodecahedron, confined within the sphere, the symbol of the universe ? He spent a dozen hours in his cell with his slate and the problem, and no other companion than a vase of water and a piece of dry bread. Then he was taken into a room to face the assembled novices. Under these circumstances the order had been passed round that they should ridicule without pity the wretched youth, who, hungry and sullen, stood before them like a culprit. " So this is the new philosopher," they would say. " How inspired he looks! He will now tell us of his meditations. Do not conceal from us what you have discovered. You will in the same way go through all the symbols in turn. A month of this *régime* and you will have become a great sage!"

At this point the master would attentively observe the young man's attitude and expression. Irritated by his fast, overwhelmed with these sarcastic words, and humiliated at not being able to solve an incomprehensible problem, no small effort was needed to control himself. Some would weep with rage, others gave sarcastic replies, whilst others again, unable to control themselves, dashed their slate madly to the ground and burst out in imprecations against school, master, and disciples alike. Then Pythagoras came forward and calmly said that, as they had failed in the test of self-respect, they were begged not to return to a school of which they had so bad an opinion, in which friendship and respect for the masters should be the most elementary of virtues. The rejected candidate would shamefacedly retire and sometimes become a redoubtable enemy of the order, like the well-known Cylon who, later on, excited the people against the Pythagoreans and brought about their downfall. On the other hand, those who bore everything with firmness, and gave just and witty replies to the provoking words they listened to, declaring they were ready to repeat the test a hundred times if only they could attain to the least degree of wisdom, were solemnly welcomed into the novitiate and received the enthusiastic congratulations of their new companions.

FIRST DEGREE—PREPARATION

The novitiate and the Pythagorean life

Then only began the novitiate called the *preparation* (paraskeia), which lasted at least two years, and might be prolonged to five. The novices, or *listeners* (akousikoi), during the lessons they received, were subjected to the rule of absolute silence. They had no right either to offer any objection to their masters or to discuss the teaching they were absorbing. This latter they were to receive with respect and to meditate upon at length. To impress this rule in the mind of the new listener, he was shown the statue of a woman, enveloped in a long veil, her finger raised to her mouth, *The Muse of Silence.*

Pythagoras did not regard youth as being capable of understanding the origin and the end of things. He thought that exercising them in logic and reasoning, before inculcating in them the meaning of truth, made them ignorant and assuming sophists. His idea was to develop in his pupils, before everything else, intuition, that primordial and superior faculty of mankind. To do this, he did not teach anything mysterious or difficult. Starting from natural sentiments, the first duties of man on entering life, he showed their relations with the laws of the universe. Whilst first of all inculcating in youth parental love, he magnified this sentiment by assimilating the idea of father to that of God, the mighty creator of the universe. "Nothing is more venerable," he said, "than the quality of fatherhood. Homer named Jupiter king of the gods, but in order to show forth all his greatness, he called him the Father of gods and men." He compared the mother to generous and beneficent Nature; as heavenly Cybele produces the stars and Demeter gives birth to the fruits and flowers of the earth, so does the mother feed the child with every joy. Accordingly the son ought to honour in his father and mother the representatives, the earthly images, of these mighty divinities. He also showed that the love of fatherland comes from the affection one feels in childhood for one's mother. Parents are given to us, not by chance, as is commonly believed, but in accordance with a previous, a superior order, called Fortune or Necessity. To honour them is *an obligation;* but a friend *must be chosen.* The novices were invited to form themselves into couples, according to their several affinities. The younger should seek in the elder the virtues he is himself aiming after, and the two companions should encourage each other towards a better life. " A friend is another self; he must be honoured as a god," said the master. Though the Pythagorean rules imposed on the " listener " novice absolute submission to his masters, it gave him full liberty in enjoying the charms of friendship, it even made of this latter the stimulus of every virtue, the poetry of life, the path leading to the ideal.

Individual energy was thus roused, morality became poetical and instinct with life, a rule lovingly accepted ceased to be a constraint, it became the very affirmation of an individuality. It was the wish of Pythagoras that obedience should be an assent and an approval. Besides this, the moral prepared the way for the philosophical teaching.

The relations set up between social duties and the harmonies of the kosmos gave one a glimpse into the law of universal agreement and analogy. In this law dwells the principle of the Mysteries, of occult teaching and of the whole of philosophy. The mind of the pupil thus grew accustomed to find the impress of an invisible order on visible realities. General maxims and concise prescriptions opened out perspectives of this superior world. Morning and evening the *Golden Verses* rang in the pupil's ear :

" First worship the immortal Gods, as they are established and ordained by the Law.
Reverence the Oath, and next the Heroes, full of goodness and light."

In commenting on this maxim, it was shown that the gods, though apparently different, were really the same among all people, since they corresponded with the same intellectual and soul forces active throughout the universe. The sage could consequently honour the gods of his own country, whilst forming of their very essence a different idea from that generally held. Tolerance for every cult; unity of people in one humanity; unity of religions in esoteric science : these new ideas became vaguely outlined in the mind of the novice like glorious divinities one might catch a glimpse of in the splendour of the setting sun. And the golden lyre continued its lofty teachings :

"Honour likewise the terrestrial Dæmons by rendering them the worship lawfully due to them."

Besides these lines the novice saw beaming as through a veil the divine Psyche, the human soul. The heavenly pathway shone like a stream of light, for in the worship of heroes and demi-gods, the initiate saw the doctrine of the future life and the mystery of universal evolution. This secret was not revealed to the novice, but he was made ready for its understanding by being told of a hierarchy of beings superior to humanity, its guides and protectors, called heroes and demi-gods. It was also stated that they served as intermediaries between man and divinity, that by their help he might step by step succeed in drawing nearer to them if he practised heroic and divine virtues. "But how could communication be obtained with these invisible spirits ? Whence comes the soul ? Whither does it proceed ? Wherefore the sombre mystery of death ?" The novice dared not formulate these questions in words, but his looks revealed them, and the only reply his masters gave him was to point to the strugglers on earth, the statues in the temple, and the glorified souls in heaven, " in the fiery citadel of the god " to which Hercules had attained.

At the foundation of the ancient mysteries, all the gods were included in the only supreme God. This revelation, including all its consequences, became the key of the Kosmos. This was the reason it was entirely reserved for initiation, properly so called. The novice knew nothing of this, he was only permitted to catch a faint glimpse of this truth from what he was told of the powers of Music and Number. " Numbers," said the master, " contain the secret of things, and God is universal harmony." The seven sacred modes, built up on the seven notes of the heptachord, correspond to the seven colours of light, to the seven planets, and to the seven modes of existence reproduced in all the spheres of material and spiritual life from the smallest to the greatest. The melodies of these modes when skilfully fused should tune the soul and make it sufficiently harmonious to vibrate in accord with the accents of truth.

With this purification of the soul corresponded of necessity that of the body, which was obtained by means of hygiene and strict moral discipline. The first duty of initiation was to overcome one's passions. He who has not harmonized his own being cannot reflect divine harmony. And yet the ideal of the Pythagorean life contained nothing of asceticism in it, for marriage was looked upon as sacred. Chastity, however, was recommended to the novices, and moderation to the initiates, as being a source of strength and perfection : " Only yield to voluptuousness when you consent to be less than yourself," said the master. He added that voluptuousness exists only in itself, comparing it " to the song of the Sirens who disappear when one approaches them, to find in their place nothing but broken bones and bleeding flesh on a wave-beaten rock, whilst true joy is like the concert of the Muses, leaving celestial harmony behind in the soul." Pythagoras believed in the virtues of the woman initiate, he greatly mistrusted the untrained woman. On a disciple asking him when he might be permitted to approach a woman he replied in ironical accents : " When you are tired of your peace of mind."

The Pythagorean day was spent in the following manner. As soon as the sun's glorious orb rose above the blue waves of the Ionian sea, gilding the columns of the Temple of the Muses, above the abode of the initiates, the young Pythagoreans chanted a hymn to Apollo, the while performing a

sacred, dignified dance. After the obligatory ablu-
tions, they proceeded in silence to the temple. Each
awakening is a resurrection possessed of its flower
of innocence. The soul must retire within itself at
the beginning of the day and remain unsullied for
the morning lesson. In the sacred wood, groups
were formed round the master or his interpreters
and the lesson was given beneath the fragrance of
the mighty trees or the shade of the porticoes. At
noon, prayer was offered to the heroes and benevo-
lent spirits. Esoteric tradition affirmed that good
spirits preferred to approach the earth with the radiance of the sun, whilst evil spirits haunted the
shades and filled the air when night came on. The
frugal midday meal generally consisted of bread,
honey, and olives. The afternoon was devoted to
gymnastic exercises, then to study and meditation,
afterwards to some mental work on the morning's
lesson. After the sun had set, prayer was offered
in common, a hymn sung to the gods of the Kosmos, to heavenly Jupiter, to Minerva, Providence,
and to Diana, guardian of the dead. Meanwhile
storax, manna, or incense were burning on the altar
in the open air, and the hymn, mingling with the
perfume, rose gently in the twilight, whilst the
early stars pierced the pale azure sky. The day
ended with the evening meal, after which the

6

youngest member read aloud, comments being made thereon by the eldest.

Thus the day passed like a limpid spring, clear as a cloudless morn. The year was divided according to the great astronomical events. Thus the return of hyperborean Apollo and the celebration of the Mysteries of Ceres saw novices and initiates of every degree, both men and women, assembled together. Young girls played on ivory lyres, married women, in purple and saffron-coloured cloaks, performed alternate choruses, accompanied by songs, along with the harmonious movements of strophe and antistrophe, imitated later on in tragedy. In the midst of these great *fêtes*, at which a divine presence was manifested in grace of form and movement and the penetrating melody of the choruses, the novice was conscious of a kind of presentiment of occult forces, the all-powerful laws of the animated universe, the deep, transparent heavens. Marriages and funeral rites were of a more intimate, but none the less solemn, character. There was one original ceremony, calculated to strike the imagination. When a novice, of his own accord, left the institute to take up once more the ordinary every-day life, or when a disciple had betrayed a secret of the doctrine, an occurrence which happened only once, the initiates raised a tomb for him in the consecrated precincts, as though he were dead. The master said : " He is more dead than the dead, for he has returned to an evil life; his body appears among men, but his soul is dead; let us weep for it!" This tomb erected to a living man, persecuted him like his own phantom, like an evil omen.

SECOND DEGREE—PURIFICATION [1]

Numbers—Theogony

It was a happy day, " a day of gold," as the ancients said, when Pythagoras received the novice into his dwelling and solemnly welcomed him into the rank of his disciples. First of all he entered into direct and connected relations with the master; he came into the inner court of his dwelling reserved for his faithful followers. Hence the name of *esoteric* (those from within) in opposition to that of *exoteric* (those from without). The real initiation now began.

This revelation consisted of a complete, rational exposition of occult doctrine, from its principles as contained in the mysterious science of numbers to the final consequences of universal evolution, the destiny and end of divine Psyche, the human soul.

[1] *Katharsis* in Greek.

This science of numbers was known under different names in the temples of Egypt and Asia. As it afforded a key to the whole doctrine, it was carefully concealed from the people. The figures and letters, the geometric forms and human representations, which served as signs in this algebra of the occult world, were understood by none but the initiate. He divulged their meaning to the adepts only after receiving from them the oath of silence. Pythagoras formulated this science in a book he wrote with his own hand, called *hieros logos* (the sacred word). This book has not come down to us, but we are acquainted with its principles from the subsequent writings of the Pythagoreans, Philolaus, Archytas, and Hierocles, the dialogues of Plato, and the treatises of Porphyry and Iamblichus. The reason they have remained a dead letter for modern philosophers is that their meaning and bearing can only be understood by comparison with all the esoteric doctrines of the East.

Pythagoras called his disciples mathematicians, because his higher teaching began by the doctrine of numbers. These sacred mathematics, however, or science of principles, were both more transcendent and more living than profane mathematics, which alone are known to our savants and philosophers. In them Number was not regarded as an abstract quantity but as the intrinsic and active virtue of the supreme One, of God the source of universal harmony. The science of *numbers* was that of the living forces, *of the divine faculties* in action in the universe and in man, in the macrocosm and in the microcosm.——In examining them, distinguishing and explaining their working, Pythagoras was evolving nothing less than a rational theogony or theology. In a real theology we should look for the principles of every science; it will be the science of God only if it shows the unity and concatenation of the sciences of nature. It deserves its name only on condition it constitutes the organ and the synthesis of all the rest. Now this is exactly the part played in the Egyptian temples by the science of the holy Word, formulated and made exact by Pythagoras under the name of the science of numbers. It claimed to supply the key of being, of science, and of life. The adept, under the guidance of his master, had to begin by contemplating its principles in the light of his own intelligence, before following its many applications in the concentric immensity of the spheres of evolution.

A modern poet has had a presentiment of this truth in causing Faust to descend to *the Mothers* to restore life to the phantom of Helen. Faust seizes the magic key, the earth melts away beneath him, he becomes unconscious and plunges into the void of space. Finally he reaches the Mothers who keep watch over the first forms of the mighty All, and cause beings to issue from the mould of the archetypes. These Mothers are the Numbers of Pythagoras, the divine forces of the world. The poet has communicated to us the thrill of his own thought before this plunge into the abyss of the Unfathomable. For the ancient initiate, in whom the direct view of intelligence was gradually aroused as though it were a new sense, this inner revelation seemed rather an ascent into the incandescent sun of Truth, whence he contemplated in the fulness of light the forms and beings thrown out in the whirl of lives by a vertiginous irradiation.

He did not reach in a single day that inner possession of truth in which man realizes universal life by the concentration of his faculties. Years of training were needed, and that agreement, so difficult to effect, of the intelligence and the will. Before using the creative word—and how few succeed in this !—one must spell out the sacred logos, letter by letter, syllable by syllable.

Pythagoras was in the habit of giving this teaching in the Temple of the Muses. This temple had been built by the magistrates of Croton at his express request and according to his plans, in an enclosed garden near his abode. The disciples of the second degree came there alone with the master. Inside this circular temple were the marble statues of the nine Muses. Standing in the centre the solemn and mysterious Hestia, covered with a veil, kept watch. Her left hand afforded protection to the fire on the hearth, whilst with her right she pointed to heaven. Both Greeks and Romans looked upon Hestia, or Vesta, as the guardian of the divine principle present in all things. The soul of sacred fire, she has her altar in the temple of Delphi, at the Prytaneum of Athens, as well as on the humblest hearth. In the sanctuary of Pythagoras she symbolized divine and central Science, or Theogony. In a circle around her, the esoteric Muses bore, in addition to their traditional and mythological names, that of the occult sciences and sacred arts of which they had the guardianship. *Urania* presided over astrology and astronomy; *Polyhymnia* over the science of souls in the other life and the art of divination; *Melpomene*, with her tragic mask, over the science of life and death, of transformations and re-births. These three superior Muses constituted together the cosmogony, or heavenly physics. *Calliope, Clio,* and *Euterpe* presided over the science of man, or psychology, with its corresponding arts, medicine, magic, and moral philosophy.

The last group, *Terpsichore, Erato,* and *Thalia,*
embraced terrestrial physics, the science of
elements, stones, plants, and animals.

Thus at a glance the organism of the sciences,
following that of the universe, appeared to the
disciple in the living circle of the Muses, illumined
by the divine flame.

After leading his disciples into this small
sanctuary, Pythagoras opened the book of the
Word, and began his esoteric teaching.

"These Muses," he said, "are only the earthly
images of the divine powers whose immaterial and
sublime beauty you will contemplate each one in
himself. Just as they have their eyes fixed upon
the fire of Hestia, from which they spring and
which gives them movement, rhythm, and melody
—so you must plunge into the central fire of the
universe, into the divine spirit, to mingle with it in
its visible manifestations." Then with bold, powerful hand, Pythagoras carried away his disciples
from the world of forms and realities; he effaced
time and space and took them with him down into
the great Monad, into the presence of the increate
Being.

Pythagoras called it the first One in which existed
harmony, the masculine Fire traversing everything,
the Spirit which moves by itself, the Indivisible and

mighty non-Manifested of which the ephemeral worlds manifest the creative thought, the Only, the Eternal, the Unchangeable, concealed beneath the many things which pass away and change. " Essence in itself escapes man," said Philolaus, the Pythagorean. " He knows only the things of this world in which the finite combines with the infinite. And how can he know them? for between things and himself there is a harmony and relation, a common principle; and this principle is given them by the One who gives to them along with their very essence, measure and intelligibility. It is the common measure between subject and object, the reason of things by which the soul participates in the final reason of the One." [1] But how can one approach It, the inconceivable Being? Has any one ever seen the Master of time, the Soul of the suns, the Spring of intelligences? No; and it is only by mingling with it that one penetrates its

[1] In transcendent mathematics it is demonstrated algebraically that zero multiplied by infinity is equal to One. Zero, in the order of absolute things, signifies the indeterminate Being. The Infinite, the Eternal in the language of the temples, was marked by a circle of a serpent biting its tail, signifying the Infinite moving itself. Now, once the Infinite is determined it produces all the numbers it contains in its great unity, and which it governs in perfect harmony.

Such is the transcendent meaning of the first problem of the Pythagorean theogony, the reason which brings it to pass that the great Monad contains all the small ones, and that all the numbers spring from the great Unity in movement.

essence. It is like an invisible fire placed in the centre of the universe, its nimble flame circulating throughout the worlds and moving the circumference. He added that it was the work of initiation to draw near the great Being, by resembling it, by making oneself as perfect as possible, dominating things by intelligence, thus becoming active like it, and not passive like them. " Is not your being, your soul, a microcosm, a small universe? Still, it is full of storm and discord. Well, the thing to do is to realize therein unity in harmony. Then and then only will God descend into your consciousness, and you will share in his power and make of your will the hearth-stone, the altar of Hestia, the throne of Jupiter !"

God, the indivisible substance, has accordingly for number the Unity which contains the Infinite, for name, that of Father, Creator, or Eternal-Masculine, and for sign, the living Fire, symbol of the Spirit, essence of the Whole. This is the first of the principles.

But the divine faculties are like the mystic lotus which the Egyptian initiate, lying in his tomb, sees emerging from the blackness of the night. At first it is only a shining spot, then it opens like a flower, and the glowing centre expands like the thousand leaves of a rose of light.

Pythagoras said that the great Monad acts as a creative *Dyad*. Immediately God manifests himself, he is double; indivisible essence and divisible substance; active, animating, masculine principle, and passive, feminine principle, or animated plastic matter. Accordingly the Dyad represented the union of the Eternal-Masculine and the Eternal-Feminine in God, the two essential and corresponding divine faculties. Orpheus had poetically expressed this idea in the line :

Jupiter is the divine Bridegroom and Spouse.

All polytheisms have intuitively been conscious of this idea, representing the Divinity under the masculine, sometimes under the feminine form.

This living, eternal Nature, this mighty Spouse of God, is not only the terrestrial but also the celestial nature, invisible to our eyes of flesh, the Soul of the world, the primordial Light, in turn Maia, Isis or Cybele, who, first vibrating beneath the divine impulse, contains the essences of all souls, the spiritual types of all beings. Then it is Demeter, the living earth, and all earths with the bodies they enfold in which these souls have come to be incarnated. Afterwards it is Woman, the companion of Man. In humanity Woman represents Nature, and the perfect image of God is not Man alone, but Man and Woman. Hence their invincible and fascinating, their fatal attraction, the intoxication of Love, in which the dream of infinite creations has play, and the dim presentiment that the Eternal-Masculine and the Eternal-Feminine enjoy perfect union in the bosom of God. " Honour be to Woman, on earth as in heaven," said Pythagoras and all the initiates of old. " She enables us to understand that mighty Woman, Nature. May she be the sanctified image of Nature and help us to mount gradually to that great Soul of the World which gives birth, preserves and renews, to divine Cybele who bears along the people of souls in her mantle of light."

The Monad represents the essence of God, the Dyad, his generative and reproductive faculty. The latter brings the world into being, the visible unfolding of God in time and space. Now the real world is triple. For just as man is composed of three elements, which are distinct though blended in one another, body, soul, and spirit; so the universe is divided into three concentric spheres : the natural, the human, and the divine world. The *Triad* or *ternary law* is accordingly the constitutive life of things and the real key to life. It is met with at every step on the ladder of life, from the constitution of the organic cell through the physiological constitution of the animal body, the working of the blood and the cerebro-spinal systems, right on to the super-physical constitution of man, to that of the universe and of God. Thus, as by enchantment, it opens up to the amazed spirit the inner structure of the universe, shows the infinite correspondences of the microcosm and the macrocosm. It acts like a light, passing into things to make them transparent, lighting up small and great worlds like so many magic lanterns.

Let us explain this law by the essential correspondence of man with the universe.

Pythagoras affirmed that the mind of man, or the intellect, takes from God its immortal and invisible, its absolutely active, nature. For the mind is that which moves itself. He defined the body as being its mortal, divisible, and passive part, and thought that what we call *soul* is closely united to the mind, though formed of a third intermediate element, coming from the *cosmic fluid*. The soul, therefore, resembles an ethereal body which the spirit weaves and builds for itself. Without this ethereal body, the material body could not be purified, it would be only an inert and lifeless mass.[1] The soul possesses a form like that of the body it vivifies, and which it survives after dissolution or death. Then, as

[1] Doctrine identical with that of the initiate St. Paul, who speaks of the *spiritual body*.

Pythagoras expresses it, in terms repeated by Plato, the *subtile chariot* either carries off the spirit to divine spheres or allows it to fall back into the dusky regions of matter, according as it is more or less good or bad. The constitution and evolution of man is repeated in ever-increasing circles over the whole scale of beings and in every sphere. Just as the human Psyche struggles between the spirit which attracts and the body which holds it back, so also humanity evolves between the natural and animal world into which it plunges by reason of its earthly roots, and the divine world of pure spirits, its heavenly source, towards which it aspires to rise. And what happens in humanity happens in all lands and solar systems in ever differing proportions, ever new modes. Extend the circle to infinity, and, if you can, form one single concept of the limitless worlds. What will you find there? The creative thought, the astral fluid, and worlds in evolution: the spirit, soul, and body of divinity. Raising veil after veil and fathoming the faculties of this divinity itself, you will there see Tryad and Dyad clothing themselves in the dull depths of the Monad, like an efflorescence of stars in the abyss of immensity.

From this rapid outline some estimate may be formed of the great importance Pythagoras attached to the ternary law, which may be said to form the corner-stone of esoteric science. All the mighty religious initiators have been conscious of it, every theosophist has had a presentiment of the same. An oracle of Zoroaster says as follows:

> The number three reigns everywhere in the universe,
> The Monad is its principle.

The incomparable merit of Pythagoras consists in having formulated it with all the clearness of Greek genius. He made of it the centre of his theogony and the foundation of the sciences. Already veiled in the exoteric writings of Plato, though altogether misunderstood by subsequent philosophers, this conception, in modern times, has been comprehended by only a few rare initiates of the occult sciences.[1] Henceforth may be seen what a broad and solid basis the law of the universal ternary offered to the classification of sciences, and to the building up of cosmogony and psychology.

Just as the universal ternary is concentrated in the unity of God or in the Monad, so the human ternary is concentrated in the conscience of the ego and in the will which gathers together in its living

[1] In the first rank of these must be placed Fabre d'Olivert (*Vers dorés de Pythagore*). This living conception of the forces of the universe, traversing it from top to bottom, has nothing to do with the *thesis*, the *antithesis* and the *synthesis* of Hegel, which are simply *jeux d'esprit*.

unity all the faculties of body, soul, and spirit. The human and divine ternary, summed up in the Monad, constitutes the *sacred Tetrad*. But it is only relatively that man realizes his own unity. His will which acts over the whole of his being cannot, however, act fully and simultaneously in its three organs, *i. e.* in instinct, soul, and intellect. The universe and God himself appear to him only in turns, successively reflected by these three mirrors :—1. Seen through instinct and the kaleidoscope of the senses, God is multiple and as infinite as his manifestations. Hence polytheism where the number of the gods is unlimited.—2. Seen through the reasonable soul, God is double, *i. e.* matter and spirit. Hence the dualism of Zoroaster, the Manichaeans, and several other religions.—3. Seen through pure intellect, he is threefold, *i.e.* spirit, soul and body in all the manifestations of the universe. Hence the trinitarian cults of India (Brahma, Vishnu and Siva) and the trinity of Christianity (Father, Son and Holy Ghost).—4. Conceived of by the will which sums up the whole, God is one, and we have the Hermetic monotheism of Moses in all its rigour. Here there is no longer personification or incarnation, we leave the visible universe and return to the Absolute. The Eternal alone rules over the world, now reduced to dust. The diversity of religions, accordingly, comes from the fact that man realizes divinity only through his own being which is relative and finite, whilst God is continually realizing the unity of the three worlds in the harmony of the universe.

This final application would alone demonstrate the—in some way—magic virtue of the *Tetragram* in the order of ideas. In it was found not only the principles of the sciences, the law of beings and their mode of evolution, but also the very reason of the different religions and their superior unity. This was in reality the universal key. Hence the enthusiasm with which Lysis speaks of it in the *Golden Verses;* one can now understand why the Pythagoreans swore by this great symbol :

> " I swear it by him who has transmitted into our souls the Sacred Quaternion, the source of nature, whose cause is eternal."

Pythagoras carried a great deal farther the teaching of numbers. In each of them he defined a principle, a law, an active force of the universe. He said, however, that the essential principles are contained in the first four numbers, since all the others are formed by adding or multiplying them. In the same way the infinite variety of beings composing the universe is produced by the combina-

7

tions of the three primordial forces: matter, soul, spirit, under the creating impulse of the divine unity which mingles and differentiates, concentrates and separates. Along with the chief masters of esoteric science Pythagoras attached great importance to the numbers seven and ten. *Seven*, the compound of three and four, signifies the union of man and divinity. It is the figure of the adepts, of the great initiates, and, since it expresses the complete realization in all things through seven degrees, it represents the law of evolution. The *number ten* formed by the addition of the first four numbers, and containing the former number, is the perfect number, *par excellence*, for it represents all the principles of divinity, evolved and re-united in a new unity.

On finishing the teaching of his theogony, Pythagoras showed his disciples the nine Muses, personifying the sciences, grouped three by three, presiding over the triple ternary evolved in nine worlds, and forming, along with Hestia, the divine science, guardian of the primordial Fire—*the sacred Decad.*

THIRD DEGREE—PERFECTION [1]

*Cosmogony and psychology.—The evolution
of the soul.*

The disciple had received the principles of science
from his master.   This first initiation had dispelled
the dense scales of matter which covered the eyes of
his spirit.   Tearing away the shining veil of mythology, it had removed him from the visible world to
cast him blindly into boundless space and plunge
him into the sun of Intelligence, whence Truth
beams forth over the three worlds.   The science of
numbers, however, was nothing but the beginning
of the great initiation.   Armed with these principles, he had now to descend the heights of the
Absolute and plunge into the depths of nature,
there to lay hold of the divine thought in the formation of things and the evolution of the soul through
the worlds.   Esoteric cosmogony and psychology
touched the greatest mysteries of life as well as
dangerous and jealously-guarded secrets of the
occult arts and sciences.

For this reason Pythagoras loved to give these
lessons, when the profane light of day had disappeared, at night by the sea-side, on the terraces of

[1] In Greek : *Teleiôtes.*

the Temple of Ceres, before the gentle murmur of the Ionian sea with its melodious cadence, and beneath the distant phosphorescence of the starry kosmos; or else in the crypts of the sanctuary where a gentle steady light was given by Egyptian lamps of naphtha. Female initiates were present at these night meetings. At times, priests or priestesses from Delphi or Eleusis came to confirm the master's teachings by relating their experiences or through the lucid words of clairvoyant sleep.

The material and the spiritual evolution of the world are two inverse movements, though parallel and concordant along the whole scale of being. The one can be explained only by the other, and, considered together, they explain the world. Material evolution represents the manifestation of God in matter by the soul of the world which works out matter. Spiritual evolution represents the working out of consciousness in the individual monads and their attempts, through the cycle of lives, to rejoin the divine spirit from which they emanate. To see the universe from the physical or from the spiritual point of view is not considering something different, it is looking at the world by the two opposite ends. From the terrestrial point of view, the rational explanation of the world ought to begin by material evolution, for it is this side of it which appears to us, but by enabling us to see the work of the universal spirit in matter and to follow up the development of the individual monads, it insensibly leads on to the spiritual point of view and causes us to pass from the without to the within of things, from the reverse of the world to its face side.

This, at any rate, was the procedure of Pythagoras, who regarded the universe as a living being, animated by a great soul and filled with a mighty intelligence. The second part of his teaching began with the cosmogony.

If we relied on the divisions of the heavens we find in the exoteric fragments of the Pythagoreans, this astronomy would be similar to that of Ptolemy; the earth motionless and the sun with the planets and the whole of the firmament turning round it. The very principle of this astronomy, however, warns us that it is purely symbolical. In the centre of his universe Pythagoras places Fire (of which the sun is only a reflection). Now in the whole of Eastern esoterism, Fire is the representative sign of Spirit, of divine, universal Consciousness. What our philosophers generally take as the natural philosophy of Pythagoras and Plato is accordingly nothing else than an imaged description of their secret philosophy, clear and light-giving to initiates, but all the more impenetrable by the mass of people as it was considered to be simple natural philosophy. We must consequently seek therein a kind of cosmography of the life of souls and nothing else. The sublunary region designates the sphere in which terrestrial attraction operates and is called the circle of generation. Initiates mean by this that for us the earth is the region of corporeal life. Here take place all the operations accompanying the incarnation and dis-incarnation of souls. The sphere of the six planets and of the sun responds to ascending categories of spirits. Olympus, conceived as a rolling sphere, is called the heaven of the stationary, because it is assimilated to the sphere of perfect souls. This infantile astronomy accordingly masks a conception of the spiritual universe.

Everything, nevertheless, inclines us to believe that the initiates of old, and especially Pythagoras, had far more correct notions of the physical universe. Aristotle positively affirms that the Pythagoreans believed in the movement of the earth around the sun. Copernicus asserts that the idea of the rotation of the earth on its axis came to him whilst reading, in Cicero, that a certain Hycetas of Syracuse had spoken of the daily motion of the earth. Pythagoras taught the double movement of the earth to his disciples of the third degree. Without having the exact measurements of modern science, he knew, as did the priests of Memphis, that the planets which come from the sun turn around it; that the stars are so many solar systems governed by the same laws as ours, and that each has its place in the immense universe. He also knew that each solar world forms a small universe which has its correspondence in the spiritual world and its own heaven. The planets served to mark the scale thereof. Still, these notions which would have overthrown popular mythology, and would have been set down by the people as sacrilegious, were never entrusted to popular writing. They were taught only under the seal of profound secrecy.[1]

The visible universe, said Pythagoras, the

[1] Certain strange definitions, in metaphorical form, which have been handed down to us and come from the secret teaching of the master, give us some idea, in their occult signification, of the magnificent conception Pythagoras had of the Kosmos. Speaking of the constellations, he called the Great and the Little Bear the hands of Rhea-Kybele. Now Rhea-Kybele means, esoterically, the rolling astral light, the divine spouse of universal fire, or of the creative Spirit, which, becoming concentrated in the solar systems, attracts the immaterial essences of beings, seizes them, and forces them into the whirl of lives. He called the planets the dogs of Proserpine. This strange expression has only an esoteric meaning. Proserpine, the goddess of souls, presided over their incarnation in matter. Pythagoras accordingly called the planets the dogs of Proserpine because they keep and retain the incarnated souls, just as the mythological Cerberus guards the souls in the infernal regions.

heavens with all their stars, are only a passing form of the soul of the world, of the great Maia who concentrates the scattered matter in the infinitudes of space and then dissolves it and scatters it in an imponderable cosmic fluid. Each solar vortex possesses a fragment of this universal soul, which evolves in its bosom for millions of centuries with a special force of impulse and measure. As regards the powers and kingdoms, the species and the living souls which appear successively in the constellations of this little world, they come from God, descending from the Father; that is to say, they emanate from an immutable and superior spiritual order, as well as from a former material evolution, I mean an extinct solar system. Of these invisible powers, some, which are altogether immortal, direct the formation of this world, the others await its unfolding in cosmic sleep or in divine dream, to return into visible generations, according to their rank and in obedience to eternal law. All the same, the solar soul and its central fire, moved directly by the great Monad, works the matter into a state of fusion. The planets are daughters of the sun. Each of them, elaborated by the forces of attraction and rotation inherent in matter, is endowed with a semi-conscious soul issuing from the solar soul; it has its distinct character, its special *rôle* in evolution. As each planet is a different expression of the thought of God, as it exercises a special function in the planetary chain, the ancient sages have identified the names of the planets with those of the great gods who represent the divine faculties in action in the universe.

The *four elements*, of which the constellations and all beings are formed, designate four graduated states of matter. The first, being the densest, is the one most refractory to spirit; the last, being the most refined, shows great affinity for spirit. *Earth* represents the solid state; *water,* the liquid state; *air*, the gaseous state, and *fire,* the imponderable state. The fifth, the *etheric* element, represents a state of matter so fine and vivid that it is no longer atomic, and possesses the property of universal penetration. It is the original, cosmic fluid, the astral light or soul of the world.

Afterwards Pythagoras spoke to his disciples of the earth's revolutions, according to the traditions of Egypt and Asia. He knew that the earth, in a state of fusion, was first surrounded by a gaseous atmosphere which, becoming liquefied by successive coolings, had formed the seas. As was his wont, he summed up this idea metaphorically by saying that the seas were produced *by the tears of Saturn* (cosmic time).

And now the kingdoms appear, and invisible germs, floating in the ethereal *aura* of the earth, whirl about in its gaseous robe and are then attracted to the deep bosom of the ocean and over the first continents that pierce their way to the surface. The vegetable and animal worlds, still in confusion, appear almost at the same time. Esoteric teachings admit of the transformation of animal species, not only in accordance with the secondary law of selection, but also by the primary law of the percussion of the earth by celestial powers, and of all living beings by intelligible principles and invisible forces. When a new species appears on the globe, the reason is that a race of souls of a superior type is being incarnated at a given epoch in the descendants of the former species, to cause it to mount a step in the ladder of evolution by moulding it afresh and transforming it into its image. Thus the esoteric doctrine explains the appearance of man on earth. From the point of view of terrestrial evolution, man is the latest branch, the crown of all the former species. But this point of view is no more sufficient to explain his entrance on to the stage of life, than it would be to explain the appearance of the first sea-weed or the first crustacean in the depths of the sea. All these successive creations infer, as does each birth, the percussion of the earth by the invisible powers which create life. That of man infers the previous reign of a celestial humanity presiding over the unfolding of terrestrial humanity, and sends it, like the waves of a formidable tide, fresh torrents of souls which become incarnate in its womb and cause to shine forth the first beams of a divine light in that bold, impulsive, terrified being who, though only just freed from the darkness of animality, is forced, in order to live, to struggle with all the powers of nature.

Pythagoras had obtained in Egyptian temples clear notions as to the mighty revolutions of the globe. The Indian and Egyptian teachings spoke of the existence of the ancient austral continent which had produced the red race and a powerful civilization, called by the Greeks, the Atlantides. They attributed the alternate emergence and immersion of continents to the oscillation of the poles and acknowledged that humanity had thus passed through six deluges. Each interdiluvian cycle brings about the predominance of a great human race. In the midst of the partial eclipses of civilization and human faculties, there is a general ascending movement.

Here we have humanity constituted and the races launched in their career through the cataclysms of the globe. But on this globe which, at birth, we take as being the immutable base of the world and which itself is carried along floating in space, on these continents which emerge from the seas to disappear afresh, amid these passing peoples, these crumbling civilizations, what is the mighty and poignant, the eternal mystery? This is the great inner problem, that of each and all, the problem of the soul which discovers in itself an abyss of darkness and light, regarding itself with a mixture of delight and terror and saying to itself: " I am not of this world, for it is not sufficient to explain me. I do not come from earth and I am going elsewhere. Where?" That is the mystery of Psyche, the mystery containing all the rest.

The cosmogony of the visible world, said Pythagoras, has led us to the history of the earth, and the latter to the mystery of the human soul. With it we touch the sanctuary of sanctuaries, the holy of holies. Once its consciousness aroused, the soul becomes for itself the most astonishing of sights. But even this consciousness is only the enlightened surface of its being, in which it suspects there to be dark and unfathomable abysses. In its unknown depths, the divine Psyche contemplates with fascinated look all lives and worlds, past and present, and the future joined to them by Eternity. " Know thyself, and thou shalt know the universe of the gods." Such was the secret of the sages and initiates. To penetrate through this narrow door into the immensity of the invisible universe, let us awake in ourselves direct vision of the purified soul, and arm ourselves with the torch of intelligence, with the science of the sacred principles and numbers.

Pythagoras thus passed from physical cosmogony to spiritual cosmogony. After the evolution of the earth, he told of that of the soul through the different worlds. Outside of initiation, this doctrine is known under the name of *transmigration of souls*. Regarding no part of secret doctrine has there been more false reasoning than here, to such an extent indeed that ancient and modern literature are acquainted with it only through puerile travesties. Plato himself, who more than any other philosopher contributed to the popularizing of the doctrine, has only given fantastic and at times extravagant glimpses of it, either because prudence or his oath of secrecy prevented him from telling all he knew. Few now doubt the fact that it must have had for initiates a scientific aspect, opening up endless perspectives and affording divine consolation to the soul. The doctrine of the ascensional life of the soul through series of existences is the common feature of esoteric traditions and the crown of theosophy. I will add that it is of the utmost importance to us. For the man of the present day rejects with equal scorn the abstract and vague immortality of philosophy and the childish heaven of an infant religion. And yet he abhors the dryness and nothingness of materialism. Unconsciously he aspires to the consciousness of an *organic immortality* responding at once to the demands of his reason and the indestructible needs of his soul. Besides, it can well be understood why the initiates of the ancient religions, though they were acquainted with these truths, kept them so secret. They are of a nature to turn the minds of those untrained to receive them. They are closely allied to the profound mysteries of spiritual generation, of sex and generation by flesh, on which hang the destinies of future humanity.

It was therefore with a kind of dread that the supreme hour for this esoteric teaching was awaited. Through the words of Pythagoras, as by some slow incantation, heavy matter seemed to lose its weight, the things of earth became transparent, those of heaven visible to the spirit. Golden and azure spheres, furrowed with luminous essence, unfolded their orbs right into the infinitudes of space.

The disciples, both men and women, grouped round the master in a subterranean part of the Temple of Ceres called the crypt of Proserpine, listened with throbbing emotions to *the celestial history of Psyche.*

What is the human soul? A portion of the mighty soul of the world, a spark of the divine spirit, an immortal monad. Still, though its possible future opens out into the unfathomable splendours of divine consciousness, its mysterious dawn dates back to the origin of organized matter. To become what it is in present-day humanity, it must have passed through all the reigns of nature, the whole scale of beings gradually developing through a series of innumerable existences. The spirit which fashions the worlds and condenses cosmic matter into enormous masses manifests itself with varying intensity and an ever greater concentration in the successive reigns of nature. A blind and confused force in the mineral, individualized in the plant, polarized in the sensations and instincts of animals, it stretches towards the conscious monad in this slow elaboration; and the elementary monad is visible in the most inferior of animals. The animal and spiritual element accordingly exists in every kingdom, though only in infinitesimal quantities in the lower kingdoms.

The souls which exist in the state of germs in the lower kingdoms stay there without moving away for immense periods of time, and it is only after great cosmic revolutions that, in changing planets, they pass to a higher reign. All they can do during a planet's period of life is to mount a few degrees. Where does the monad begin? As well ask at what hour a nebula was formed or a sun shone for the first time. Anyhow, what constitutes the essence of any man must have evolved for millions of years through a chain of lower planets and kingdoms, keeping through all these existences an individual principle which follows it everywhere. This obscure but indestructible individuality constitutes the divine seal of the monad in which God wills to manifest himself through consciousness.

The higher one ascends in the series of organisms, the more the monad develops the principles latent in it. Polarized force becomes capable of sensation, capacity of sensation becomes instinct, and instinct becomes intelligence. In proportion as the flickering flame of consciousness is lit, this soul becomes more independent of the body, more capable of existing freely. The fluid, non-polarized soul of minerals and vegetables is bound to the elements of earth. That of animals, strongly attracted by terrestrial fire, stays there for some time after leaving its body, and then returns to the surface of the globe to re-incarnate in its species without ever having the possibility of leaving the lower layers of the air. These are peopled with elementals or animal souls which play their part in atmospheric life and have a great occult influence over man. The human soul alone comes from the sky, and returns there after death. At what period of its long cosmic existence has the elementary become the human soul? Through what incandescent crucible, what ethereal flame has it passed? The transformation has been possible in an interplanetary period only by the meeting of human souls already fully formed which have developed in the elementary soul its spiritual principle and have impressed their divine prototype like a seal of fire in its plastic substance.

But what journeys and incarnations, what planetary cycles must still be traversed for the human soul thus formed to become the man we are acquainted with! According to the esoteric traditions of India and Egypt, the individuals of whom mankind at present consists, began their human existence on other planets, in which matter is far less dense than our own. Man's body was then almost vaporous, his incarnations light and easy. His faculties of direct spiritual perception

8

were evidently very powerful and subtile in this first human phase; reason and intelligence on the other hand were in an embryonic condition. In this half-corporeal, half-spiritual state, man saw spirits, everything was full of splendour and charm to his eyes, full of music to his ears. He could hear the harmony of the spheres. He neither thought nor reflected, scarcely even willed, but simply lived, drinking in sounds, forms and light, floating like a dream from life to death and from death to life. It was this that the Orphic poems called *the heaven of Saturn*. It is only by becoming incarnate on planets ever denser and denser that man became materialized, according to the doctrine of Hermes. By becoming incarnate in denser matter, humanity has lost its spiritual sense, but by an ever-increasing struggle with the outside world, it has powerfully developed its reason, intelligence and will. The earth is the last rung of this descent into matter which Moses calls the exit from paradise, and Orpheus, the fall into the sublunary circle. From these depths man can, with difficulty, re-ascend the circles in a series of new existences and regain his spiritual faculties by the free exercise of his intellect and will-power. Then only, say the disciples of Hermes and Orpheus, does man acquire by his *action* the consciousness and the possession of the divine; then only does he become the *son of God*. Those who have borne this name on earth must, before appearing among us, have descended and remounted the dreadful spiral.

Then what is the humble Psyche at its origin? A passing breath, a floating germ, a wind-swept bird, migrating from life to life. And yet, after innumerable lapses, and millions of years, it has become the daughter of God and no longer recognizes any other home than heaven! This is why Greek poetry, so profound and luminous in its symbolism, compared the soul sometimes to the winged insect, sometimes to the earth-worm, and again to the heavenly butterfly. How often has it been a chrysalis, and how often a winged creature of light? Though it will never know this, it still feels that it has wings!

Such is the vertiginous past of the human soul. It affords us an explanation of its present condition and enables us to glimpse into its future.

What is the position of divine Psyche in earth life? The slightest reflection suffices to show us that we could not imagine a stranger or more tragic one, since being painfully roused to consciousness in the dense atmosphere of earth, the soul has entwined itself in the folds of the body. Only through it does the soul live, breathe, and think, and yet it is not the body. In proportion as it develops, it feels increasing within itself a quivering light, something invisible and immaterial which it calls its spirit, its conscience. Yes, man has an innate sentiment of his triple nature, for, even in his instinctive language, he distinguishes his body from his soul, and his soul from his spirit. The soul, however, captive and troubled, struggles between its two companions as between the thousand twining folds of a serpent and an invisible genius calling it, whose presence, however, can only be felt by passing gleams and the beating of his wings. At times this body absorbs it to such an extent that it is only through its passions and sensations that the soul lives; with the body it rolls in the blood-stained orgies of anger or the dense mist of carnal pleasures, until, of its own accord, it becomes terrified by reason of the profound silence of its invisible companion. Then again, attracted by the latter, it rises to such lofty heights of thought, that it forgets the existence of the body until a peremptory call reminds it of its presence. And yet an inner voice tells it that between itself and the invisible guest the bond cannot be broken, whilst death will break its connection with the body.

Tossed to and fro between the two in an eternal struggle, the soul seeks in vain for happiness and truth. In vain does it seek to find itself in passing sensations, in fugitive thoughts, in the world which changes like a mirage. Finding that nothing is lasting, troubled and driven about like a leaf in the wind, it has doubts of itself and of a divine world which is only revealed to it by its own pain and the impossibility it feels of reaching this world. Human ignorance is written in the contradictions of pretended sages, and human sadness in the unfathomable hunger of the human glance. Finally, whatever the range of his knowledge, birth and death shut in man between two fatal bounds. These are two gates of darkness, beyond which he sees nothing. The flame of his life is lit as he enters the one and extinguished as he leaves the other. Can it be so with the soul? If not, then what becomes of it?

Many have been the replies which philosophers have given to this poignant problem. In its essence that given by theosophical initiates of all times is the same. It is in accord with universal feeling and the inner spirit of religions. The latter has expressed the truth only under superstitious or symbolical forms. The esoteric doctrine opens up far wider perspectives; its affirmations are strictly related to the laws of universal evolution. This is what initiates, instructed by tradition and by the

many experiences of psychic life, have said to man :
That which is restless in thyself, which thou callest
thy soul, is an ethereal double of the body which
contains in itself an immortal spirit. The spirit
builds and forms for itself, by its own activity, its
spiritual body. Pythagoras calls it *the subtile
chariot of the soul*, because it is destined to remove
it from earth after death. *This spiritual body is
the organ of the spirit*, its sensitive envelope and
instrument of volition ; it serves to animate the body,
which would otherwise remain inert. In apparitions of the dying or the dead, *this double* becomes
visible, under circumstances, however, which always
presuppose a special nervous condition of the seer.
The degree of fineness, power and perfection of the
spiritual body varies according to the quality of
the spirit which it contains, and between the substance of souls woven in the astral light, though
impregnated with the imponderable fluids of earth
and heaven, there are more numerous distinctions,
greater differences than between all earthly bodies
and all states of ponderable matter. This astral
body, though far finer and more perfect than the
earthly one, is not immortal as is the monad which
it contains. It changes and becomes purified
according to its different environments. The spirit
is perpetually moulding and transforming it into

its own image; it never leaves it however, though it unrobes itself of it by degrees; it is continually clothing itself with more ethereal substances. This was the teaching of Pythagoras, who could not conceive of abstract spiritual entity, the formless monad. Spirit in itself, whether in the far-away sky or on earth, must have an organ; that organ is the living soul, whether bestial or sublime, obscure or radiant, retaining, however, the human form, the image of God.

What happens at death? When the final hour approaches, the soul generally has a presentiment of its coming separation from the body. It sees over again its earthly existence in abridged scenes rapidly succeeding one another and of startling clearness. When the exhausted life stops in the brain, the soul becomes perplexed and altogether loses consciousness. If it is holy and pure, its spiritual senses have already been aroused by gradual detachment from matter. Before dying, in some way or other, if only by the introspection of its own state, it has already felt the presence of another world. Beneath the silent, distant appeals, the vague beams of the Invisible, earth has already lost its consistence, and when the soul finally leaves the cold corpse, rejoicing in its deliverance, it feels itself carried away into a glorious light, towards the spiritual family to which it belongs. It is not so, however, with the ordinary man, whose life has been divided between material instincts and higher aspirations. He awakes in a state of semi-consciousness, as though in the torpor of a nightmare. No longer has he an arm to stretch forth or a voice to cry out with; still, he remembers and suffers, existing, as he does, in a limbus of darkness and terror. All that he sees is the body from which he is detached, but for which he still feels an invincible attraction. It is for it that he lived; and now, what is it? In terror he looks for himself in the icy fibres of his brain, in the stagnant blood of his veins, and no longer finds himself. Is he dead or living? He would like to see, to hold on to something, but he cannot see, he can take hold of nothing. Darkness is all around, chaos within. He sees only one thing, and this thing attracts and terrifies him at the same time—the sinister phosphorescence of his own earthly tenement; and the nightmare recommences.

This state may be prolonged for months or years. Its duration depends on the strength of the material instincts of the soul. Still, good or evil, infernal or celestial, this soul will gradually become conscious of itself and of its new condition. Once free from its body, it will escape into the abysses of the terrestrial atmosphere, whose electric streams carry it here and there, and whose many-shaped inhabitants, wandering about, more or less like itself, it is beginning to perceive, like fugitive flashes in a thick mist. Then there begins a desperate, vertiginous struggle on the part of the soul, which is still dull and heavy, to rise into the upper strata of the air, to free itself from earthly attraction and reach, in the heaven of our planetary system, the region proper to it and which friendly guides alone can show it. But before this can take place, a long period must often intervene. This phase of the life of the soul has borne different names in religions and mythologies. Moses called it Horeb; Orpheus, Erebus; Christianity, Purgatory, or *the Valley of the Shadow of Death*. The Greek initiates identified it with the cone of shadow which the earth is always trailing behind it, which shadow reaches as far as the moon; for this reason they called it the *abyss of Hecate*. In these mirky depths, say the disciples of Orpheus and of Pythagoras, are tossed to and fro the souls which make desperate efforts to reach the circle of the moon, though the violence of the winds beats them back to earth by thousands. Homer and Virgil compare them with whirling leaves, or swarms of birds maddened by the tempest.

The moon played an important part in ancient esoterism. On its surface, facing the heavens, the souls were regarded as purifying their astral body before continuing their celestial ascent. It was also supposed that heroes and great spirits took up their abode for a time on the portion of its surface turned towards the earth, in order to clothe themselves in bodies appropriate to our world before reincarnation. There was attributed to the moon, in a certain measure, the power to magnetize the soul for earthly incarnation, and to demagnetize it for its heavenly abode. In a general way, these assertions, to which initiates attached a meaning that was at once real and symbolical, signified that the soul must pass through an intermediary stage of purification and free itself from the impurities of earth before continuing its journey.

In what terms can one describe the arrival of the pure soul into its own world? The earth has disappeared like a dream. A fresh sleep, a delightful swoon now envelops it as in a caressing embrace. All that it now sees is its winged guide carrying it away with lightning rapidity into the depths of space. What can we say of its awakening in the vales of some ethereal star, devoid of elemental atmosphere, where everything—mountains, flowers and vegetation—is of an exquisite, sensitive and

eloquent nature? Above all else, what can one say
of those luminous forms, men and women, sur-
rounding it like a sacred procession, to initiate it
into the sacred mystery of its new life? Are they
gods or goddesses? No; they are souls like itself;
the wonder consists in the fact that their inmost
thoughts beam forth in their countenance, that
tenderness and love, desire or fear radiate through
those diaphanous bodies in a scale of luminous
colorations. Here, body and countenance are no
longer the mask of the soul; the transparent soul
appears in its real form, shining forth in the clear
light of unpolluted truth. Psyche has returned to
her divine home. The secret light in which she
laves herself, which emanates from her and returns
in the smile of beloved ones; this light of great
felicity is the soul of the world wherein she
is conscious of the presence of God! No more
obstacles now! She will love and know; she will
live with no other limit than her own desire to soar.
Strange and marvellous happiness! She feels that
strong, profound affinities unite her to all her companions. For in the life beyond, those who do not
love flee from one another; those alone meet
together who understand one another. With them
she will celebrate the divine mysteries in more
beautiful temples, in a more perfect communion.

These will be living poems, ever new, each soul of
which will be a strophe, and each one will live
again its life in that of others.　Then, quivering with delight, she will spring forth into the
radiance on high, to the call of the Messengers, the
winged Spirits, those who are called Gods, for they
have escaped the circle of generations.　Led on by
these sublime intelligences, she will try to decipher
the great poem of the Secret Word, to understand
what she can grasp of the symphony of the
universe.　She will receive hierarchical information
from the circles of Divine Love; she will endeavour
to see the Essences which the animating Spirits
scatter throughout the worlds; she will contemplate
the glorified Spirits, living rays of the God of Gods,
but without being able to bear their blinding glory
which makes suns look pale as smoky lamps!
Then, when she returns terrified from these
dazzling flights—for she shudders in presence
of such immensities—she will hear from afar
the call of beloved voices, and will fall back on the
golden strands of her star, beneath the rose-coloured
veil of a billowy sleep, peopled with forms clothed
in white, and filled with sweet perfumes and melodious strains.

Such is the heavenly life of the soul, scarcely
conceived of by our earth-clouded minds, but

divined by initiates, lived by seers and demonstrated by the law of analogy and universal concordance. In vain do our rude imagery and imperfect language attempt to translate it; each living soul, however, feels the germ of this life in its hidden depths. Though in our present condition it is impossible for us to realize it, the philosophy of occultism has formulated its psychical conditions. The idea of ethereal constellations, invisible to us, though forming part of our solar system and serving as an abode for happy souls, is often found in the secrets of esoteric tradition. Pythagoras calls it a counterpart of the earth : the *antichthone*, lit up by the central Fire, *i.e.*, by the divine light. At the end of the *Phaedo*, Plato describes this spiritual land at some length, though in disguised fashion. He says that it is as light as air, and is surrounded by an ethereal atmosphere. In the other life, we see that the soul preserves the whole of its individuality. Of its terrestrial existence it retains none but noble memories, leaving the others to fall into that forgetfulness which the poets called the waves of Lethe. Freed from all defilement, the human soul feels its consciousness restored, so to speak. From without the universe, it has come back to within it; Cybele-Maïa, the soul of the world, has, with deep yearning, drawn

it back to her bosom.   Here, Psyche will work out
her dream, that dream continually broken and ever
being recommenced on earth.   She will work it out
in accordance with her earthly effort and acquired
intelligence, but she will magnify it an hundred-
fold.   Crushed hopes will again revive beneath the
dawn of her divine life; the gloomy sunsets of earth
will kindle into the dazzling light of day.   Though
man had lived only one hour of enthusiasm or self-
denial, that single pure note, torn away from the
discordant scale of his earthly life, will be repeated
in his after-life in marvellous progressions and
æolian harmonies.   The fugitive delights that we
obtain from the enchantment of music, the ecstasy
of love or the raptures of charity are only the stray
notes of a harmony to which we shall then be
listening.   Is this simply saying that such life will
be only one long dream, one magnificent hallucination ?   What is there truer than that which the soul
feels within itself and which it realizes by its divine
communion with other souls ?   Initiates, being con-
sistent and transcendent idealists, have always
thought that the only real and lasting things on
earth are manifestations of spiritual Beauty, Love
and Truth.   As the after-life can have no other
object than this Truth, this Beauty and this Love
for those who make them the object of their lives,

they are convinced that heaven will be truer than earth.

The heavenly life of the soul may last hundreds or thousands of years, according to its degree or strength of impulse. It belongs, however, only to the perfect, to the most sublime souls, to those which have passed beyond the circle of generations, to prolong it indefinitely. The latter have not only attained to temporary rest, but to immortal action in truth; they have created wings for themselves. Being light itself, they are inviolable; seeing across the worlds, they rule them. The rest are carried along by an inflexible law to re-incarnation, in order to undergo a fresh trial, and to rise to a higher rung or to fall lower if they fail.

The spiritual, like the terrestrial life, has its beginning, its apogee and its decline. When this life is exhausted, the soul feels itself overcome with heaviness, giddiness and melancholy. An invincible force once again attracts it to the struggles and sufferings of earth. This desire is mingled with terrible dread and a mighty grief at leaving divine life. But the time has come; the law must be obeyed. The heaviness increases, a sensation of dimness is felt. The soul no longer sees its companions of light except through a veil, and this veil, ever denser and denser, gives a presentiment

of the coming separation. It hears their sad fare-
wells; the tears of the blest, the loved ones whom it
is leaving, fall over it like heavenly dew which will
leave in its heart the burning thirst of an unknown
happiness. Then—with solemn oaths—*it promises*
to remember—to remember the light when in
the world of darkness, to remember truth when in
the world of falsehood, and love when in the world
of hatred. The return, the immortal crown, can
only be acquired at this cost. It awakens in a
dense atmosphere; ethereal constellation, diaphanous souls, oceans of light—all have disappeared.
And now it is back on earth, in the abyss of birth
and death. Nevertheless, it has not yet lost its
celestial memory; the winged guide still visible to
its eyes points out the woman who is to be its
mother. The latter bears within her womb the
germ of a child, but this germ will only live if
the spirit comes in to animate it. Then for nine
months is accomplished the most impenetrable
mystery of earthly life, that of incarnation and
maternity.

The mysterious fusion operates slowly but with
perfect wisdom—organ by organ, fibre by fibre.
Accordingly as the soul plunges into that warm
cavern, which roars and swarms with life, in proportion as it feels itself caught up in the meander-

ings of the viscera with their thousand recesses and folds, the consciousness of its divine life becomes effaced and dies out. For between it and the light above are interposed waves of blood and tissues of flesh, crushing it and filling it with darkness. This distant light is already nothing more than a dying flicker. Finally, a terrible pang compresses it in a vice; a bloody convulsion tears it from the mother soul and fastens it down into a throbbing, palpitating body. The child is born, a pitiful image of earth, and he cries aloud with fright. The memory of the celestial regions however has returned to the occult depths of the Unconscious; it will only be revived either by Knowledge or by Pain, by Love or by Death !

Accordingly, the law of incarnation and dis-incarnation unfolds to us the real meaning of life and death. It constitutes the principal phase in the evolution of the soul, enabling us to follow it backwards and forwards right into the depths of nature and divinity. For this law reveals to us the rhythm and measure, the reason and object of the soul's immortality. From being abstract or fantastic, it makes it living and logical by showing the correspondences of life and death. Terrestrial birth is death from the spiritual point of view, and death is a celestial resurrection. The alternation of both

9

lives is necessary for the development of the soul, and each of them is at once the consequence and the explanation of the other. Whosoever is imbued with these truths is at the very heart of the mysteries, at the centre of initiation.

But, we shall be asked, what is there to prove for us the continuity of the soul, of the monad, the spiritual entity through all these existences, since it loses the memory of them in succession? What is there to prove, we shall reply, the identity of your person during waking existence and during sleep? You wake up every morning from a state as strange, as inexplicable as death; you rise from this condition of nothingness to return to it again at night. Was it nothingness? No, for you have been dreaming, and your dreams have been as real to you as the reality of the waking state. A change in the physiological conditions of the brain has modified the relations of soul and body and displaced your psychical point of view. You were the same individual but you found yourself in another environment, and living another existence. In magnetized subjects, somnambulists and clairvoyants, sleep develops new faculties which to us seem miraculous, though they are the natural faculties of the soul when detached from the body. Once aroused, these clairvoyants no longer remember what they have seen, said or done during their lucid sleep, but they remember perfectly well in one sleep what happened in the previous one, and at times predict with mathematical certainty what will happen in the next. They have, then, two consciousnesses as it were, two alternate lives entirely distinct from one another, but each of which has its own rational continuity. They roll themselves round the same individuality like cords of different colours round an invisible thread.

Consequently, it is in a very deep sense that the initiate poets of old called sleep *the brother of death*. A veil of forgetfulness separates the sleeping from the waking state, like birth and death, and, just as our earthly life is divided into two parts always alternating, so also the soul, in the immensity of its cosmic evolution, alternates between incarnation and spiritual life, between earth and heaven. This alternate passage from one plane of the universe to another, this reversing of the poles of its being, is no less necessary for the development of the soul than alternate waking and sleeping is necessary for the bodily life of man. When passing from one existence to the other, we need the waters of Lethe. In this present existence, a salutary veil conceals from us past and future alike. But oblivion is not complete, since light passes through the veil. Innate ideas alone prove a former existence. There is more, however; we are born with a world of vague remembrances, mysterious impulses, divine presentiments. In children born of gentle quiet parents we find outbursts of wild passions which atavism does not sufficiently explain, and which come from a former existence. Sometimes in the humblest life we find fidelity to a sentiment or an idea, altogether sublime and inexplicable. Is not this a result of the promises and oaths of the celestial life? The occult memory the soul has kept of them is stronger than all earthly reasoning. According as it attaches itself to this memory or abandons it, is it seen to overcome or to succumb. True faith consists in this mute fidelity of the soul to itself. For this reason, one may conceive that Pythagoras like all theosophists considered bodily life as a necessary elaboration of the will, and heavenly life as a spiritual growth, an accomplishment.

Lives follow without resembling one another, but a pitiless logic links them together. Though each of them has its own law and special destiny, the succession is controlled by a general law, which might be called *the repercussion of lives*.[1] In accordance with this law, the actions of one life

[1] The law called *Karma* by Brahmans and Buddhists.

have, fatally, their repercussion in the following one. Not only will man be born again with the instincts and faculties he has developed in his preceding incarnation, but the very manner of his existence will be largely determined by the good or bad use he has made of his liberty in the preceding life. There is no word or action which has not its echo in eternity, says a proverb. According to esoteric doctrine, this proverb is literally applied from one life to another. Pythagoras considered that the apparent injustice of destiny, the difformity and wretchedness of one's lot, misfortunes of every kind, find their explanation in the fact that each existence is the reward or the punishment of the former one. A criminal life engenders one of expiation, an imperfect life, one of trial. A good life determines a mission, a superior life, a perfected mission by the re-establishment of initiation and the spiritual selection of marriages. In this way races follow one another and humanity progresses. The initiates of old saw much further into the future than those of our days. They acknowledged that a time would come when the great mass of people constituting present-day humanity would pass on to another planet, there to begin a new cycle. In the series of cycles of which the planetary chain consists, the whole of humanity will develop the intellectual, spiritual and transcendent principles which great initiates have developed in themselves in this life, and will thus bring them to general fruition. It goes without saying that such a development embraces not merely thousands, but millions of years, and that it will bring about changes in human conditions such as we cannot at present form any imagination of. In expressing them, Plato says that in those times the gods will really inhabit the temples of men. It is logical to admit that in the planetary chain, *i.e.* in the successive evolutions of our humanity on other planets, its incarnations should become more and more ethereal in their nature, insensibly approaching the purely spiritual state of that eighth sphere which is outside the circle of generation, and by which the divine state was denoted by theosophists of old. It is also natural that, as all do not start from the same point, and many loiter on the way or fall back, the number of the elect should continually diminish in this marvellous ascent. Our earth-limited intelligences are dazed by this conception, but heavenly intelligences contemplate it without the least fear, just as we regard a single life. Is not the evolution of souls, thus understood, in conformity with the unity of the Spirit, the principle of principles; with the

homogeneity of Nature, the law of laws; and with
the continüity of movement, the force of forces?
Seen through the prism of spiritual life, a solar
system does not constitute a material mechanism
only, but a living organism, a celestial kingdom in
which souls travel from world to world like the very
breath of God animating it.

What then is the final end of man and humanity,
according to esoteric doctrine? After so many
lives, deaths, re-births, periods of calm and poignant awakings, is there any limit to the labours of
Psyche? Yes, say the initiates, when the soul has
definitely conquered matter, when, developing all
its spiritual faculties, it has found in itself the
principle and end of all things, then, incarnation
being no longer necessary, it will enter the divine
state by a complete union with the divine intelligence. Since we have scarcely any presentiment
of the spiritual life of the soul after each earthly
life, how shall we form any idea of this perfect
life which must follow the whole series of its
spiritual existences? This heaven of heavens will
be to all former happiness as the ocean is
to a river. In the mind of Pythagoras, the apotheosis of man was not a plunge into unconscious-
ness, but rather creative activity in supreme
consciousness. The soul which has become pure

spirit does not lose its individuality, but rather perfects it as it rejoins its archetype in God. It remembers all its former existences, which it regards as so many ladders to reach the point at which it embraces and penetrates the universe. In this state, man is no longer man, as Pythagoras said, but demi-god. For in his entire being he reflects the ineffable light with which God fills immensity. For him, knowledge is power; love is creation; being is radiating truth and beauty.

Is this a definite limit? Spiritual eternity has other measures than solar time, though it, too, has its stages, norms, and cycles. They entirely transcend human conception, however. Still, the law of progressive analogy in the ascending scale of nature allows of our affirming that the spirit, once it has reached this sublime state, can no longer return, that though the visible worlds change and pass away, the invisible world, which is its *raison d'être*, its source and basis, and of which the divine Psyche forms a part, is immortal.

It was in such a brilliant perspective that Pythagoras ended the history of the *divine Psyche*. The last word had died away on the lips of the sage, but the meaning of that incommunicable truth remained suspended in the motionless air of the crypt. Each listener believed that he had finished the dream of lives, and was awaking to life in the mighty peace and boundless ocean of the one life. The naphtha lamps quietly lit up the statue of Persephone, standing there in the character of a heavenly reaper; they revived her symbolical history in the sacred frescoes of the sanctuary. At times, a priestess who had entered a state of ecstasy under the harmonious voice of Pythagoras seemed to incarnate in her attitude and the radiance of her countenance the unspeakable beauty of the vision she saw. Then, the disciples—seized with a thrill of religious emotion—looked on in silence. Soon, however, the master, with a slow commanding gesture, brought back to earth the inspired prophetess. By degrees the tension of her features was relieved, she sank back into the arms of her companions and fell into a profound lethargy, from which she awoke troubled and sorrowful, and apparently exhausted after her heavenly flight.

Then, leaving the crypt they mounted to the gardens of Ceres just as morning was beginning to dawn over the sea, and the stars to disappear from mortal sight.

FOURTH DEGREE—EPIPHANY

*The adept.—The woman initiate.—Love
and marriage.*

With Pythagoras we have now reached the summit of initiation in ancient times. From these heights the earth appears drowned in shadow, like a dying star. Sidereal perspectives open out— and the vision from on high, the epiphany of the universe,[1] is unfolded before one's wondering gaze in its entirety. The object of his instruction, however, was not the absorption of man in contemplation or ecstasy. The master had brought his disciples into the unmeasurable regions of the Kosmos, plunging them into the abyss of the invisible. After this terrifying journey, the true initiates were to return to earth better, stronger and more prepared for the trials of life.

The initiation of the intelligence was to be followed by that of the will, the most difficult of all. The disciple had now to become imbued with truth in the very depths of his being, to put it into prac-

---

[1] The *epiphany*, or vision from above; the *autopsy*, or direct vision; the *theophany*, or manifestation of God, are so many correlative ideas and divers expressions to indicate the state of perfection in which the initiate, having united his soul to God, contemplates truth in its entirety.

tice in everyday life. To attain to this ideal, one must, according to Pythagoras, unite three kinds of perfection: the realization of truth in intelligence, of virtue in soul and of purity in body. This latter was to be maintained by a prudent system of hygiene and a well-balanced chastity. This was demanded not as an end but as a means to an end. All bodily excesses leave marks, impurities, so to speak, in the astral body, the living organism of the soul, and consequently in the mind. For the astral body participates in all the acts of the physical body; indeed, it is the former which gives effect to them, the material body being, without it, nothing but an inert mass. Accordingly the body must be pure for the soul to be pure also. Then the soul, continually enlightened by the intelligence, must acquire courage, self-denial, devotion and faith, in a word, virtue, by which a second nature must be made to replace the first. Finally, the intellect must reach wisdom through knowledge, so that in everything it may be able to distinguish good from evil and see God in the smallest of beings as well as in the immensity of worlds. On reaching these heights, man becomes an adept; and, if he possesses sufficient energy, he enters into possession of new faculties and powers. The inner senses of the soul expand,

and the senses of the body are dominated by the
radiant will. His bodily magnetism, penetrated
by the potency of his astral soul, electrified
by his will, acquires an apparently miraculous
power. At times he cures the sick by the laying
on of hands or simply by his presence. His
look alone often penetrates the thoughts of
men. Sometimes, in the waking state, he sees
events taking place afar off.[1] He acts at a distance

[1] I will here mention two well-known facts of this kind, which
are quite authentic. The first belongs to antiquity, its hero being
the famous philosopher-magician, Apollonius of Tyana.

1. *Second sight of Apollonius of Tyana.*—'' Whilst these things
(the assassination of the Emperor Domitian) were taking place
at Rome, Apollonius saw them at Ephesus. Domitian was assailed
by Clement about noon; on the very same day, at that moment,
Apollonius was discoursing in the gardens close to the Xystes.
Suddenly he lowered his voice as though smitten with sudden
terror. He continued his speech, but his language was of a
different character, as is the case often with those who are speaking or thinking of something else. Then, he stopped, as though
he had lost the thread of his argument, gave a terrified look on
the ground, took three or four steps forward and exclaimed :
' Strike the tyrant !' One would have said that he saw, not
the image of the deed in a mirror, but the deed itself in all its
reality. The Ephesians (for the whole of Ephesus was present at
the speech of Apollonius) were struck with wonder. Apollonius
stopped like a man waiting to see the result of some doubtful
event. Finally he exclaimed : ' Be of good courage, Ephesians,
the tyrant has been killed to-day. To-day? Yes, by Minerva ! He
was being assassinated the very moment I interrupted my speech.
The Ephesians thought that Apollonius had lost his senses; it was
their keen desire that he should have said what was true, but they
were afraid that some danger might come to them as the result
of this speech. . . . Soon, however, messengers came bringing

by the concentration of thought and will on such
persons as are attached to him by bonds of personal

---

the good news and testifying in favour of the knowledge of
Apollonius, for every detail: the murder of the tyrant, the day
of its consummation, the hour of noon, the instigator of the
murder whom Apollonius had encouraged, were found to be in
perfect conformity with those the Gods had shown him on the
day of his discourse to the Ephesians."—*Life of Apollonius*, by
Philostratus.

2. *Second sight of Swedenborg.*—The second fact refers to the
greatest seer of modern times. The objective reality of Swedenborg's visions may be discussed, but there can be no doubt regarding his second sight, which has been attested by a multitude of
facts. Swedenborg's vision of the burning of Stockholm, a
distance of ninety miles away, caused much wonderment in the
second half of the eighteenth century. Kant, the well-known
German philosopher, caused an inquiry to be made by a friend
living at Gothenburg, in Sweden; the following is his account
as related to a lady friend—

" In my opinion the following fact is of the greatest demonstra-
tive importance, and ought to do away with any kind of doubt.
In 1759, M. de Swedenborg, one Saturday about four in the
afternoon, about the end of December, landed at Gothenburg,
after a journey to England. M. William Castel invited him to
his house, where a company of fifteen persons was present. At
six o'clock in the evening, M. de Swedenborg, who had left the
room, returned, with a look of consternation on his pallid face,
and said that ' at that very moment a fire had burst out in
Stockholm, at the Sudermalm, and was rapidly spreading its
ravages in the direction of his own home. . . . He said that the
house of one of his friends, whom he named, was in ashes, and
that his own was in danger. At eight o'clock, again leaving the
room, he returned and said joyfully: ' Thank God! The fire
has been extinguished at the third door from my own house.'
That very evening the governor was informed of the fact. On
Sunday morning, Swedenborg was summoned before this function-
ary, who questioned him on the matter. Swedenborg gave an
exact description of the fire, its beginning and end, and the time

sympathy, causing his image to appear to them as though his astral body could be transported out of his material body. The appearance of the dying or the dead to their friends affords exactly the same phenomenon. The apparition however which the dying man or the soul of the dead man generally produces through an unconscious desire, in the last few moments of life or in the second death, is generally produced by the adept when in perfect health and consciousness. Still, he can only do this during sleep, and a sleep which is almost always of a lethargic nature. Finally, the adept feels himself as it were surrounded and protected by invisible beings, superior spirits of light, who lend him their strength and aid him in his mission.

Adepts are rare, but even more rare are those

---

it had lasted. The same day, the news spread throughout the town, which was all the more excited as the governor had manifested interest in it, and many people were anxious about their property and friends. On Monday evening there arrived in Gothenburg a courier whom the business men of Stockholm had despatched during the conflagration. Among the letters the fire was described in exactly the manner above mentioned. What can be alleged against the authenticity of this event? The friend who wrote to me has examined the whole affair, not only in Stockholm, but, about two months ago, at Gothenburg also; he is well acquainted with the best-known families, and has been able to obtain complete information in a town where there are still living the majority of the eye-witnesses, considering the short lapse of time (nine years) since 1859."—Letter to Mademoiselle Charlotte de Knoblich, quoted by Matter, in his *Life of Swedenborg*.

who attain to this power.   Greece knew but three :
Orpheus at the dawn of Hellenism, Pythagoras at
its apogee, and Apollonius of Tyana in its final
decline.   Orpheus was the mighty and inspired
initiator of Greek religion; Pythagoras, the
organizer of esoteric science and the philosophy of
the schools; Apollonius, the moralizing stoic and
popular magician of the decadence.   In all three,
however, in spite of differences and degrees, there
beams the divine ray, the mind passionately inflamed for the salvation of souls, indomitable
energy clothed in gentleness and serenity.   But do
not draw too near these mighty, calm brows; a
silent fire is beneath, the furnace of an ardent but
ever restrained will.

Pythagoras accordingly represents to us an adept
of the highest type, possessed of the scientific
mind and cast in philosophic mould to which
the spirit of modern times most nearly approaches.
But he himself neither could, nor pretended to
make perfect adepts of his disciples.   A great
inspirer is always at the beginning of every
great epoch.   His disciples and their pupils
form the magnetic chain which carries his
thought out into the world.   In the fourth degree
of initiation, Pythagoras therefore contented himself with teaching his followers how to apply his

doctrine to life. The *Epiphany*, the vision from above, set forth an ensemble of profound, regenerating views on things of earth.

The origin of good and evil remains an incomprehensible mystery for whomsoever has not taken into account the origin and the end of things. A morality which does not consider the final destiny of man will be merely utilitarian and very imperfect. Besides, human liberty does not really exist for such as always feel themselves the slaves of their passions, nor does it by right exist for such as believe neither in the soul nor in God, for whom life is a lightning flash between two states of darkness. The first live in the servitude of the soul, enchained by the passions; the latter in the slavery of intelligence limited to the physical world. It is not so for the religious man, or for the true philosopher, nor with much greater reason for the theosophist initiate who realizes truth in the trinity of his being and the unity of his will. To understand the origin of good and evil, the initiate regards *the three worlds* with the spiritual eye. He sees the murky world of matter and animalism in which inevitable *Destiny* holds sway. He sees the luminous world of the Spirit which, for us, is the invisible world, the immense hierarchy of liberated souls who are themselves *Providence* in action, the world where divine law reigns. Between the two he catches a dim glimpse of humanity, the lower elements of which plunge into the natural world whilst the higher ones touch the divine spheres. The genius and spirit of humanity is *Liberty*; for the moment man perceives truth and error, he is free to choose, to associate with Providence in accomplishing truth, or, by following error, to fall beneath the law of destiny. The act of will joined to that of intelligence is nothing but a mathematical point, but from this point springs forth the spiritual universe. Every spirit partially feels by instinct what the theosophist totally understands by his intellect: that Evil is what causes man to descend to the fatality of matter, and that Good is what makes him rise towards the divine law of the Spirit. His true destiny is to be ever rising higher, and that from his own efforts. But to do this he must also be free to descend again to the very lowest. The circle of liberty widens out to the infinitely great in proportion as one ascends, it shrinks to the infinitely small in proportion as one descends. The higher one rises, the freer he becomes; for the more one enters into light, the more power for good he acquires. And the more one descends, the more enslaved does he become; for each fall into evil diminishes the intelligence of

10

the true and the capacity for good. Destiny
accordingly reigns over the past, Liberty over the
future, and Providence over both, *i.e.* over the
ever-existing present, which may be called
Eternity.[1]   From the combined action of Destiny,
Liberty and Providence spring the innumerable
destinies, the hells and the paradises of souls.
Evil, being discord with divine law, is not the
work of God but that of man, and has only a
relative, an apparent and transitory existence.
Good, being accord with divine law, alone really
and eternally exists.   Neither the priests of Delphi
and Eleusis, nor the initiate philosophers would ever
reveal these profound thoughts to the people, who
might have misunderstood and misused them.   In
the Mysteries this doctrine was symbolically represented by the mutilation of Dionysos, though what
was called *the sufferings of God* was hidden from
the profane by an impenetrable veil.

The greatest of all religious and philosophical
discussions deal with the question of the origin of
good and evil.   We have just seen that esoteric

---

[1] This idea springs logically from the human and divine ternary,
from the trinity of the microcosm and the macrocosm we have
spoken of in the previous chapters.   The metaphysical correlation
of Destiny, Liberty and Providence has been admirably drawn
by Fabre d'Olivert, in his commentary on the *Golden Verses of
Pythagoras.*

teachings hold the key to this question. There is another important question on which the social and political problem depends: *the inequality of human conditions*. In the very spectacle of evil and pain there is something terrifying. Their apparently arbitrary and unjust distribution may be said to be the origin of all hatred, revolt and denial. Here again the profound esoteric teaching brings into our earthly darkness its sovereign light of peace and hope. The diversity of souls, conditions and destinies can indeed only be justified by plurality of existences and the doctrine of reincarnation. If man is born for the first time into this life, what explanation can be given of the innumerable evils which seem to fall on him as the effect of chance? How can it be admitted that there is such a thing as eternal justice, when some are born under conditions which fatally bring about misery and humiliation, whilst others are born fortunate and live the happiest of lives? If, however, it is true that we have lived other lives, and shall do so again after death, that through all these existences there reigns the law of recurrence and repercussion —then the differences of soul, of condition and destiny, will be nothing but the results of previous lives and the manifold applications of this law. Differences of condition spring from an unequal employment of liberty in past lives, and intellectual differences from the fact that men belong to extremely different degrees of evolution, which range from the semi-animal condition of retrogressing races to the angelic states of saints and the divine kingship of genius. In reality earth resembles a vessel, and all we who inhabit it are travellers coming from far-away lands, dispersing, by degrees, in every direction of the compass. The doctrine of reincarnation gives a *raison d'être*, in accordance with eternal justice and logic, for the most terrible suffering as well as for the most envied happiness. The idiot will now be understood by us if we think that his dull, stupid condition, of which he is half conscious and from which he suffers, is the punishment for a criminal use of his intelligence in another life. All the degrees of physical and moral suffering, of happiness and misfortune in their innumerable varieties, will appear to us as the natural and wisely-graduated blossomings of the instincts and actions, the faults and virtues of a long past, for in its occult depths the soul retains everything it accumulates in its divers existences. According to hour and influence, the former births reappear and disappear, and destiny, or rather the spirits who control it, proportion the soul's kind of reincarnation to its degree and quality.   Lysis expresses this truth, beneath a veil, in the *Golden Verses*—

> "Thou wilt likewise know, that men draw upon themselves their own misfortunes voluntarily, and of their own free choice. Unhappy that they are! They neither see nor understand that their good is near them."

Far from weakening the sentiment of brotherhood and of the solidarity of all men, such teaching is bound to strengthen it. We owe help, sympathy and charity to all; for we are all of the same race, though we have reached different stages. All suffering is sacred, for pain is the test of the soul. All sympathy is divine, for it enables us to feel, as by a magnetic thrill, the invisible chain binding together all the worlds. The virtue of grief is the reason of genius. Sages and saints, prophets and divine creators shine with more resplendent beauty in the eyes of those who know that they too come forth from universal evolution. How many lives, what innumerable victories have been needed to acquire this might which fills us with wonder? What heavens have already been traversed to bring to us this innate light of genius? We know not; but these lives have been lived, these heavens do exist. The conscience of nations is not mistaken; the prophets have not lied in calling these men the sons of God, messengers from heavenly places. Their mission is demanded by eternal Truth, they are protected by invisible legions and the living Word speaks in them !

There is one difference in men springing from the primitive essence of individuals, and another, as we have just said, coming from the degree of spiritual evolution to which they have attained. From this latter point of view, we see that men may be placed in four classes, comprising every subdivision and degree.

1. In the great majority of men, the will acts especially in the body. These may be designated as *instinctive* persons. Their sphere includes not only physical work, but also the exercise and development of the intelligence in the physical world, consequently commerce and industry.

2. In the second degree of human development the will, and consequently the consciousness, has its abode in the soul, *i. e.* in sensitiveness, reacted on by intelligence, which constitutes understanding. These are *animic, or passionate persons.* According to temperament, they are fitted to become warriors, artists or poets. The great majority of savants and literary men belong to

this class. They live in relative ideas, modified by passions or limited by a fixed horizon, without rising to the height of pure Idea or Universality.

3. In a third class of men, a far rarer one, the will has acquired the habit of acting principally in pure intellect, of setting free the intelligence, in its special function, from the tyranny of the passions and of the limits of matter, thus giving all their conceptions a character of universality. These are the *intellectual* persons. They include such heroes as perish in martyrdom for their country, the highest type of poets, and especially true philosophers and sages, those whose mission it is, according to Pythagoras and Plato, to govern humanity. In these men, passion is not extinct; for without it nothing could be effected; it constitutes fire and electricity in the moral world. The passions have here become the servants of intelligence, whilst in the former category intelligence is, oftener than not, the slave of the passions.

4. The loftiest human ideal is realized by a fourth class of men, those who have added to the dominion of the intelligence over soul and instinct, that of the will over their whole being. They exercise supreme mastery through the control and possession of all their faculties. In the human

trinity they have realized unity. Owing to this marvellous concentration, which collects together all the powers of life, their will, by projecting itself into others, acquires an almost limitless strength, a radiating and creative magic. These men have borne different names in history. They are primordial men, *adepts, great initiates*, sublime geniuses who transform and metamorphose humanity. So rare are they that they may be counted in history; Providence scatters them here and there at long intervals of time, like stars in the heavens.[1]

Evidently this last category is outside of all rule or classification, still, such a constitution of human society as takes no account of the first three categories, without granting each its normal function and the means needed for self-development, is merely external, it is anything but *organic*. It is clear that, in primitive times, probably dating back to the Vedic epoch, the Brahmans of India founded the division of society into castes on the ternary principle. In time, however, this division, so just and fruitful a one, became changed into an

[1] This classing of men corresponds to the four stages of Pythagorean initiation, and forms the basis of all initiations, even that of the primitive freemasons, who were not without a smattering of esoteric teaching.—See Fabre d'Olivert, *les Vers dorés de Pythagore.*

aristocratic and sacerdotal privilege. The principle of vocation and initiation was replaced by that of heredity. The closed castes finally became petrified and the irretrievable decadence of India followed. Egypt, which maintained, during the rule of the Pharaohs, the ternary constitution with the movable and open castes, the principle of initiation as applied to the priesthood and that of examination and control of all military and civil functions, existed for a period ranging between five and six thousand years without a change of constitution. As for Greece, her lively, versatile temperament caused her to pass rapidly from aristocracy to democracy, and from the latter to tyranny. She turned round in this vicious circle like a sick man passing from fever to lethargy and back again to fever. Perhaps she needed this excitement to produce her unparalleled work: the translation of the profound though obscure wisdom of the East into clear, universal language; the creation of the Beautiful by Art; and the foundation of an open and reasonable science following on a secret, intuitive initiation. And none the less was she indebted to the principle of initiation for her religious organization and her loftiest inspirations. Speaking from a social and political standpoint, it may be said that she always lived in whatever was provisional and excessive. Pythagoras, in his capacity as an adept, had well understood, from the heights of initiation, the eternal principles which control society, and was following out the plan of a mighty reform in accordance with these truths. Soon we shall see how his school and himself suffered shipwreck in the storms of democracy.

From the pure, undefiled summits of his teachings the life of the worlds rolls on, in accordance with the rhythm of Eternity. Glorious epiphany! Beneath the magic rays, however, of the unveiled firmament, earth, humanity and life also unfold to us their secret depths. To feel the presence of God, the infinitely great must be recognized in the infinitely small. This is what the disciples of Pythagoras experienced when, to crown his teaching, the master demonstrated to them how eternal Truth is manifested in the union of man and woman in marriage. The beauty of the sacred numbers they had heard and contemplated in the Infinite they were about to recognize at the very heart of life, for them God was reflected in the great mystery of Sex and Love.

Antiquity had grasped an important truth which succeeding ages have too long misunderstood. Woman, effectively to fulfil her duties as wife and mother, needs special instruction and initiation. Hence a purely feminine initiation; that is to say, one reserved altogether for women. This existed in India, where in Vedic times the woman was a priestess at the domestic altar. In Egypt it dates back to the mysteries of Isis. Orpheus organized this initiation in Greece. Right on to the decay of paganism we see it flourishing in the Dionysiac mysteries as well as in the temples of Juno, Diana, Minerva and Ceres. It consisted of symbolic rites and ceremonies, in festivals by night as well as in special instruction given by aged priestesses or by the high priest, and dealing with the most private concerns of married life. Advice and regulations were given regarding the relations between the sexes, the times of the year and month favourable for healthy conception. The highest importance was attached to the physical and moral hygiene of woman during pregnancy, so that the sacred work, the creation of the child, might be accomplished in accordance with divine law. In a word, the science of conjugal life and the art of maternity were taught. The latter extended to some years after the birth of the child. Up to the age of seven, the children remained in the gynæceum—which the husband never entered—under the mother's exclusive control. The wisdom of antiquity looked upon the child as being a delicate plant, which, if it is to be kept from wasting away, needs the warm, cheering atmosphere of a mother's love. The father would stunt its growth, a mother's kiss and embrace are needed to enable it to blossom forth; a woman's mighty encircling love to protect from outside attack this soul which a new life fills with terror and dismay. It is because woman consciously fulfilled these lofty functions which antiquity regarded as divine, that she was in very truth the priestess of the family, the guardian of the sacred fire of life, the Vesta of the hearth. Feminine initiation may accordingly be regarded as the veritable reason of the beauty of the race, its robust descendants and the length of duration of the family in Greek and Roman antiquity.[1]

In establishing a section for women in his Institute, Pythagoras merely deepened and refined what already existed. The women he initiated received from him, along with rites and precepts, the final principles of their functions. In this way he bestowed the consciousness of their *rôle* on such as were deserving of it. He revealed to them the transfiguration of love in perfect marriage, which

[1] Montesquieu and Michelet are almost the only writers who have made mention of the virtue of Greek wives. Neither of them states its cause, which I point out in these few lines.

is the blending of two souls at the very centre of
life and truth. Is not man in his strength the representative of the creative spirit and principle?
And does not woman in the totality of her power
personify nature in its plastic force, its wonderful
realizations, at once terrestrial and divine? Then
if these two beings succeed in a complete mingling
of body, soul and spirit, they will form between
them an epitome of the universe. To believe in
God, however, woman needs to see him living in
man; and to effect this, man must be an initiate.
He alone, by reason of his profound knowledge of
life and creative will-power, is capable of fecundat-
ing the feminine soul, of transforming it by means
of his divine ideal. This ideal the loved one gives
him back manifold in her vibrating thoughts, her
keen sensations and profound divinations. She
sends him back his image transfigured by enthusiasm, she *becomes* his ideal, for she realizes it
by the power of love in her own soul. Through
her he becomes living and visible, he is made flesh
and blood. For if man creates through desire and
will, woman, both physically and spiritually,
brings into being through love.

In her *rôle* as lover or wife or mother or being
inspired, she is no less great and is even more
divine than man. For love is self-forgetfulness.

The woman who forgets self and loses herself in her love must ever be sublime. In such self-abasement she finds her celestial re-birth, her crown of light and the immortal radiance of her entire being.

In modern literature love has been reigning as a master for the past two centuries. This is not the purely sensual love, born of bodily beauty, as in the poetry of old, nor is it the insipid worship of an abstract and conventional ideal as in the middle ages; it is rather a love both sensual and psychic which gives full scope to its liberty and individual fancy. Oftener than not both sexes wage war in love itself. There is the revolt of the woman against man's egoism and brutality; the scorn of the man at woman's deceit and vanity, carnal exclamations and the ineffectual wrath of the victims to voluptuousness, the slaves to debauchery. With all this we find deep-rooted passions and terrible attractions, all the more powerful from being trammeled and fettered by worldly conventions and social institutions. Hence a love full of passion and storm, of moral ruin and tragic catastrophe, on which the modern novel and drama are almost exclusively based. One might say that tired man, finding God neither in religion nor in science, in despair seeks for

him in woman. And he does well, but it is only
through the initiation of the great truths that he
will find Him in Her and Her in Him. In these
souls, which know neither themselves nor one
another, which sometimes leave one another with
mutual maledictions, there is, as it were, a mighty
desire for self-penetration, for finding in such
intermingling a happiness that is impossible. In
spite of the aberrations, the outbursts of debauchery resulting therefrom, this desperate
search is necessary; it springs from an unconscious divinity. It will be a vital element in the
reconstruction of the future. For when man and
woman have found themselves and one another
through the channels of profound love and initiation, the fusion of the two will be the radiating
and creative force *par excellence*.

It is only quite recently, then, that psychic love,
the soul's love-passion, has entered into literature
and through it into universal consciousness. It
has its origin, however, in the initiation of the
past. The reason Greek literature scarcely men-
tions it, is that it was a most rare exception.
Another reason may be found in the profound
secrecy of the mysteries. And yet religious and
philosophic tradition have handed down traces of
the woman initiate. Away behind official poetry

and philosophy appear a few half-veiled though luminous woman forms. We have already mentioned Theoclea who inspired Pythagoras; later on will come Corinna, the priestess, ofttimes the fortunate rival of Pindar, who himself was the greatest initiate among the Greek lyric poets; finally, the mysterious Diotima appeared at the banquet of Plato to give the supreme revelation of Love. By the side of these exceptional *rôles* the Greek woman exercised her veritable priesthood at the fireside and in the gynæceum. Indeed, she created those heroes, artists and poets whose sublime deeds, sculptures and songs we so greatly admire. It was she who conceived them in the mystery of love, who formed them in her womb with the desire and love of beauty, who brought them to birth after protecting them beneath her motherly wings. It must be added that for the man and woman who are real initiates the creation of the child has an infinitely finer signification and greater importance than for us. When father and mother know that the soul of the child existed previous to its birth on earth, conception becomes a sacred act, the summons of a soul to submit to incarnation. Between the incarnate soul and the mother there is almost always considerable similarity. Just as evil-minded and wicked women attract spirits possessed of demons, divine spirits are attracted to gentle tender-hearted mothers. Is not this invisible soul, long waited for, which is to come and finally appears—so wonderfully and yet so surely—something divine in its nature? Painful will be its birth and imprisonment in flesh. For though a dense veil gathers between itself and the heaven it has left, though it no longer remembers—alas! it suffers none the less on that account! Sacred and divine is the task of the mother who is to create for it a fresh dwelling, to mitigate the harshness of its prison and render the trial easier to bear.

Thus we see that the teaching of Pythagoras, which had begun by the divine trinity in the profound recesses of the Absolute, ended in the human trinity at the centre of life. In Father, Mother and Child, the initiate could now recognize the Spirit, Soul and Heart of the living universe. For him this final initiation constituted the foundation of the social work, conceived of in all the height and beauty of the ideal, a building to whose construction each initiate had to bring his stone.

CHAPTER V

MARRIAGE OF PYTHAGORAS—REVOLUTION AT
CROTON—THE MASTER'S END—THE SCHOOL AND
ITS DESTINY

AMONG the women who followed the master's teaching was a maiden of great beauty. Her father, an inhabitant of Croton, was named Brontinos. His daughter's name was Theano. Pythagoras was now sixty years of age, but mastery over passion and a pure life wholly consecrated to his mission, had kept him in perfect health and strength. The youth of the soul, that immortal flame the great initiate draws from his spiritual life and nourishes on the hidden forces of nature, shone forth in him, throwing into subjection all around. The Grecian mage was not at the decline, but rather at the height of his might. Theano was attracted to Pythagoras by the almost supernatural radiance emanating from his person. Grave and reserved, she had sought from the master an explanation of the mysteries she loved though without understanding them. When,

162

however, beneath the light of truth and the tender glow which gradually enveloped her, she felt her inmost soul expand like the mystic rose with its thousand petals, when she felt that this blossoming forth came from him and his words—she silently conceived for the master a boundless enthusiasm and a passionate love.

Pythagoras had made no effort to attract her. His love and affection were bestowed on all his disciples; he thought only of his school, of Greece and the future of the world. Like many great adepts, he had denied himself the pleasures of earthly love to devote himself to his work. The magic of his will, the spiritual possession of so many souls he had formed and who remained devoted to him as to a well-loved father, the mystic incense of all those unexpressed affections which came to him, and that exquisite fragrance of human sympathy which bound together the Pythagorean brethren—all this took the place of voluptuousness, of human happiness and love. One day, as he was alone, meditating on the future of his school in the crypt of Proserpine, he saw coming to him, with grave, resolute steps, this beautiful virgin to whom he had never spoken in private. She sank on her knees at his feet, and with downcast eyes begged the master—the one who could do everything!—to set her free from an impossible, an unhappy love which was consuming her, body and soul. Pythagoras wished to know the name of the one she loved. After much hesitation, Theano confessed that it was himself, but that, ready for any sacrifice, she would submit to his will. Pythagoras made no reply. Encouraged by his silence, she raised her head with suppliant look. Her eyes seemed to contain the very essence of a life and soul offered as a sacrifice to the master.

The sage was greatly disturbed; he could overcome his senses and imagination, but the electric flash from that soul had pierced his own. In this virgin, matured by passion, her countenance transfigured by a sentiment of utter devotion, he had found his companion, and caught a faint glimpse of a more complete realization of his work. With troubled look, Pythagoras raised the maiden to her feet, and Theano saw from the master's eyes that their destinies were for ever united.

By his marriage with Theano, Pythagoras affixed *the seal of realization* to his work. The union and fusion of the two lives was complete. One day when the master's wife was asked what length of time elapsed before a woman could become pure after intercourse with a man, she replied: "If it is with her husband, she is pure all the time; if with another man, she is never pure." Many women would smilingly remark that to give such a reply one must be the wife of Pythagoras, and love him as Theano did.

And they would be in the right, for it is not marriage which sanctifies love, it is love which justifies marriage. Theano entered so thoroughly into the thought and life of her husband, that after his death she became a centre for the Pythagorean order, and a Greek author quotes her opinion as that of an authority on the doctrine of Numbers. She bore Pythagoras two sons, Arimnestes and Telauges, and a daughter Damo. At a later date Telauges became the master of Empedocles, to whom he handed down the secrets of the doctrine.

The family of Pythagoras offered the order a real model to follow. His house was called the Temple of Ceres, and his court the Temple of the Muses. In domestic and religious festivals, the mother led the women's chorus, and Damo that of the maidens. In all respects Damo was worthy of her parents. Pythagoras entrusted to her certain writings expressly forbidding her to communicate them to any one outside the family. After

the dispersion of the Pythagoreans, Damo fell
into great poverty. She was offered a large sum
for the precious manuscript, but, faithful to her
father's will, she always refused to part with it.

Pythagoras lived in Croton for thirty years.
Within twenty years this extraordinary man had
acquired such power that those who called him a
demi-god were not looked upon as exaggerating.
This power seemed to have something miraculous
about it, no like influence had ever been exercised by a philosopher. It extended not merely
to the school of Croton and its ramifications in
other towns on the coast of Italy, but even to the
politics of all these small states. Pythagoras was
a reformer in the whole acceptation of the term.
Croton, a colony of Achaïa, had an aristocratic
constitution. The *Council of the Thousand*, drawn
from the noblest families, carried on the legislative
and kept watch over the executive power. Popular
assemblies existed, though their power was re-
stricted. Pythagoras, who wished the State to be
all order and harmony, was no more enamoured
of oligarchical compression than of the chaos of
demagogy. Accepting the Doric constitution as
it was, he simply tried to introduce a fresh
mechanism into it. The idea was a bold one, for
it consisted in the creation, over and above the

political power, of a scientific one with a delibera-
tive and consultative voice in questions of vital
interest, and becoming the key-stone, the supreme
regulator of the State. Above the Council of the
Thousand, he organized the *Council of the Three
Hundred*, chosen by the former, but recruited from
among the initiates alone. The number was sufficient for the task. Porphyrus relates that two
thousand of the citizens of Croton gave up their
wonted mode of living and united in order to live
together with their wives and children after plac-
ing their possessions in one common stock. It
was thus the wish of Pythagoras that at the head
of the State there should be a scientific government, not so mysterious though quite as important
as the Egyptian priesthood. What he realized
for a short time remained the dream of all such
initiates as dealt with politics, viz. the introduc-
tion of the principle of initiation and examination
into the government of the State, and the reconcilia-
tion in this superior synthesis of the elective or
democratic principle with a government constituted of a select number of intelligent and virtuous
citizens. The result was that the Council of the
Three Hundred formed a kind of political, scientific
and religious order, of which Pythagoras himself
was the recognized head. The members were

bound to him by a solemn and an awful oath of
absolute secrecy, as was the case in the Mysteries.
These societies or ἑταιρείαι spread from Croton,
the seat of the original society, throughout almost
the whole of the towns in Greater Greece, where
they exercised a powerful political influence. The
Pythagorean order also tended to become the
head of the State throughout the whole of Southern Italy. Its ramifications extended to Tarentum, Heracleium, Metapontum, Rhegium, Himera,
Catana, Agrigentum, Sybaris and, according to
Aristoxenes, even among the Etruscans. As
regards the influence of Pythagoras on the
government of these rich and mighty cities, nothing loftier, nothing more liberal or pacific could
be imagined. Wherever he appeared, order,
justice and concord were restored. Once, when
summoned into the presence of a tyrant of Sicily,
he persuaded him, by his eloquence alone, to
restore the wealth he had unjustly acquired and to
abdicate a power he had usurped. Such towns as
were subject to one another he made independent
and free. So beneficent were his actions that
when he went into a town the inhabitants would
say: "He has not come to teach but rather to
heal."

The sovereign influence of a great mind and

character, that magic of soul and intelligence, arouses jealousy and hatred which is only the more terrible and violent because it is itself the less capable of attack. His sway lasted a quarter of a century; the reaction came when the indefatigable adept had reached the age of ninety. It began in Sybaris, the rival of Croton, where a rising of the people took place and the aristocratic party was overthrown. Five hundred exiles asked the inhabitants of Croton to receive them, but the Sybarites demanded their extradition. Dreading the anger of a hostile town, the magistrates of Croton were on the point of complying with this demand when Pythagoras intervened. At his entreaty, they refused to hand over the unhappy suppliants to their implacable enemies, whereupon Sybaris declared war upon Croton. The Croton army, however, commanded by the famous athlete, Milon, a disciple of Pythagoras, completely defeated the Sybarites. The downfall of Sybaris followed; the town was taken and plundered, utterly destroyed and converted into a wilderness of ruins. It is impossible to admit that Pythagoras could have approved of so terrible a revenge, which was altogether opposed to his principles, as, indeed, to those of all initiates. Neither he nor Milon, however, could check the unbridled passions of a conquering army, when once inflamed by long-standing jealousy and excited by an unjust attack.

Revenge, whether in individuals or in nations, always brings about a recoil of the passions let loose. The Nemesis of this vengeance was a terrible one; its consequences fell on Pythagoras and the whole of his order. After taking Sybaris, the people demanded a division of the land. Not content with obtaining this, the democratic party proposed a change of constitution, depriving the Council of the Thousand of its privileges, and suppressing the Council of the Three Hundred; they were no longer willing to admit any other authority than universal suffrage. Naturally the Pythagoreans, members of the Council of the Thousand, were opposed to a reform which was contrary to their principles and was undermining the patient work of their master. They had already become the object of that dull hatred which mystery and superiority ever arouse in the masses. Their political attitude excited the anger of the demagogy, and personal hatred against the master proved the spark which kindled the fire.

A certain Cylon had, some time before this, offered himself as a candidate for the School. Pythagoras, who was very strict in accepting disciples, refused him because of his violent and headstrong disposition. This rejected candidate became a bitter enemy. When public opinion began to turn against Pythagoras he organized a club, a large popular society in opposition to that of the Pythagoreans. He succeeded in attracting to himself the principal leaders of the people, and at the meetings hatched a revolution which was to begin by the expulsion of the Pythagoreans. Cylon rises to his feet in front of a sea of upturned excited faces and reads extracts stolen from the secret book of Pythagoras, entitled: The Sacred Word (*hiéros logos*). These extracts are then travestied and wrongly interpreted. A few of the speakers make an attempt to defend the brothers of silence, who respect even dumb animals. Such are greeted with outbursts of laughter. Cylon ascends the tribune again and again. He demonstrates that the religious catechism of the Pythagoreans is a crime against liberty. "And that is a slight charge," he adds. "Is this master, this would-be demi-god, whose least word is blindly obeyed, and who has merely a command to give, to have all his brethren exclaiming: 'The master has said it!'—any other than the tyrant of Croton, and the worst of all tyrants, an occult one? What else than scorn and disdain for the people is this indissoluble friendship which unites all the members of the Pythagorean ἑταιρεíαι composed of? They are never tired of repeating the words of Homer when he says that the prince should be the shepherd of his people. In their eyes the people are evidently nothing better than a worthless flock. The very existence of the order, I say, is a permanent conspiracy against the rights of the people. Until it is destroyed liberty will be a vain word in Croton!" One of the members of the meeting, animated by a feeling of loyalty, exclaimed: "Let Pythagoras and his followers be given an opportunity, at any rate, to justify their conduct in our presence before we condemn them." Cylon replied haughtily: "Have not these Pythagoreans deprived you of the right to judge and decide upon public matters? What right have they to ask you to listen to them now? They did not consult you when they deprived you of the right to exercise justice, now it is your turn to strike without listening to them!" Such vehement opinions were greeted with rounds of applause, and popular frenzy and passion rose higher than ever.

One evening, when forty of the principal members of the order had met at the abode of Milon, the tribune collected his followers and the house was surrounded. The Pythagoreans, who had the master with them, barricaded the doors. The enraged crowd set fire to the building, which speedily became enveloped in flames. Thirty-eight Pythagoreans, the very first of the master's disciples and constituting the flower of the order, along with Pythagoras himself, perished either in the flames or at the hands of the people. Archippus and Lysis alone escaped massacre.[1]

Thus died this mighty sage, this divine man whose effort it had been to instil his own wisdom into human rule and government. The murder of the Pythagoreans was the signal for a democratic revolution in Croton and about the Gulf of Tarentum. The towns of Italy expelled from their walls

[1] This is the version of Diogenes of Laërte regarding the death of Pythagoras—according to Dicearchus, quoted by Porphyry, the master escaped massacre, along with Archippus and Lysis. He wandered from town to town until he reached Metapontum, where he died of hunger in the Temple of the Muses. The inhabitants of Metapontum, on the other hand, affirmed that the sage they had taken in, died peacefully in their city. They pointed out to Cicero his house, seat and tomb. It is noteworthy that, long after the master's death, those cities which had persecuted Pythagoras most, at the time of the democratic change of opinion, claimed for themselves the honour of having offered him refuge and protection. The towns around the Gulf of Tarentum claimed that they each contained the ashes of the philosopher with as much desperation as the towns of Ionia disputed among one another the honour of having given birth to Homer.—See this question discussed in M. Chaignet's conscientious work: *Pythagore et la philosophie pythagoricienne*.

the unfortunate disciples of the master. The order was dispersed; fragments of it, however, spread throughout Sicily and Greece, propagating everywhere the master's words and teachings. Lysis became the teacher of Epaminondas. After fresh revolutions, the Pythagoreans were permitted to return to Italy on condition they no longer formed a political body. They were still united in a touching fraternity, and looked upon themselves as one family. One of them who had fallen upon sickness and poverty was kindly taken in by an inn-keeper. Before dying he traced a few mysterious signs on the door of the inn and said to the host: " Do not be uneasy, one of my brothers will pay my debt." A year afterwards, as a stranger was passing by this inn he saw the signs and said to the host: " I am a Pythagorean; one of my brothers died here; tell me what I owe you on his account." The order existed for two hundred and fifty years; the ideas and traditions of the master have come down to the present times.

The regenerating influence of Pythagoras over Greece was immense. This influence was exercised in mysterious though certain fashion, by means of the temples he had visited. At Delphi we have seen that he gave new might to the science of divination, strengthened the priestly influence, and by

his art formed a model Pythoness. Thanks to this
inner reform, which aroused enthusiasm in the very
heart of the sanctuaries and in the soul of the
initiates, Delphi became more than ever the moral
centre of Greece. This was especially evident
during the Median wars. Scarcely had thirty years
elapsed since the death of Pythagoras when the
Asiatic cyclone, predicted by the Samian sage,
burst out upon the coasts of Hellas. In this epic
struggle of Europe against a barbaric Asia, Greece,
representing liberty and civilization, has behind her
the science and genius of Apollo. He it is whose
patriotic and religious inspiration stirs up and
silences the springing rivalry between Sparta and
Athens. It is he, too, who is the inspirer of men
like Miltiades and Themistocles. At Marathon,
enthusiasm is so great that the Athenians believe
they see two warriors, clad in light, fighting in
their ranks. Some recognize in them Theseus and
Echetos; others, Castor and Pollux. When the
invasion of Xerxes, tenfold more formidable than
that of Darius, breaks over Thermopylæ and sub-
merges Hellas, it is the Pythoness who, on her
tripod, points out the way of safety to the envoys
from Athens, and helps Themistocles to gain the
victory at Salamis. The pages of Herodotus thrill
with her broken phrases: " Abandon the home-

steads and lofty hills if the city is built in a circle
. . . fire and dreadful Mars mounted on a Syrian
chariot will bring your towers to ruins . . . temples
are tottering in their fall, their walls are dripping
with cold sweat, whilst black blood is falling from
their pinnacles . . . depart from my sanctuary.
Let a wooden wall be your impregnable bulwark.
Flee! turn your backs on numberless enemies on
foot and on horseback! O divine Salamis! How
deadly wilt thou be to those born of woman!"[1] In
the account given by Eschylus the battle begins
with a cry resembling the pæan, Apollo's hymn:
"Soon the day, led on white coursers, spreads
throughout the world its resplendent light. Immediately a mighty shout, resembling a sacred chant,
rises from the ranks of the Greeks and the echoes
of the island respond in a thousand loud-sounding
voices." What wonder that, intoxicated with the
wine of victory, the Greeks at the battle of Mycale,
in the presence of stricken Asia, chose as a rallying
cry: "Hebe, Eternal Youth!" Yes, it is the breath

---

[1] In temple language the term *son of woman* indicated the
lower degree of initiation, woman here signifying nature. Above
these were *the sons of man* or initiates of the Spirit and the Soul,
the sons of the Gods or initiates of the cosmogonic sciences, and
the sons of God or initiates in the supreme science. The
Pythoness calls the Persians *sons of woman,* giving them this
name from the character of their religion. Interpreted literally,
her words would be devoid of meaning.

of Apollo that moves through these wonderful Median wars. Religious enthusiasm, which works miracles, carries off both living and dead, throws a dazzling light on victory, and gives a golden glory to the tomb. All the temples were plundered and destroyed, that of Delphi alone remained intact. The Persian hosts advanced to spoil the holy town. A quiver of dread came over all. The solar god, however, said through the voice of the pontiff: "I will defend myself!" Orders were given from the temple that the city be deserted, the inhabitants take refuge in the grottoes of Parnassus, and the priests alone keep sacred guard on the threshold of the sanctuary. The Persian army enters the town, all still as death; the statues alone look down as the hosts march along. A black cloud gathers at the foot of the gorge, the thunders roll and the lightning flashes on the invaders. Two enormous rocks roll down from the summit of Parnassus, crushing to death great numbers of Persians.[1] At the same time noises and shouts

[1] "These may still be seen in the enclosure of Minerva," said Herodotus, VIII. 39. The invasion of the Gauls, which took place two centuries later, was repelled in like manner. Here, too, a storm gathers, thunderbolts fall time after time on the Gauls; the earth quakes beneath their feet, they see supernatural visions; and the temple of Apollo is saved. These facts seem to prove that the priests of Delphi were acquainted with the science of cosmic fire and knew how to handle electricity by occult power as did

issue from the Temple of Minerva, flames leap from the ground beneath the very feet of the invaders. Before such wonders the barbarians fall back in terror and the dismayed army takes to flight. The god has undertaken his own defence.

Would these wonders have happened, would these victories humanity looks upon as its own have taken place, had not Pythagoras, thirty years earlier, appeared in the Delphic sanctuary to kindle there the sacred fire? This may, indeed, be questioned.

One word more regarding the master's influence on philosophy. Before his time, there had been natural philosophers on the one hand, and moral philosophers on the other; Pythagoras included in a vast synthesis, morality, science and religion. This synthesis is nothing else than the esoteric doctrine, whose full glory I have endeavoured to reveal in the very basis of Pythagorean initiation. The philosopher of Croton was not the inventor but the light-bearing arranger of these fundamental truths, in the scientific order of things. Consequently I have chosen his system as offering the most favourable framework to a complete account

---

the Chaldæan magi.—See Amédée Thierry, *Histoire des Gaulois,* I. 246.

of the doctrine of the Mysteries as well as of true theosophy.

Those who have followed the master up to this point will have seen that at the basis of the doctrine there shines the sun of the one Truth. Scattered rays may be discovered in philosophies and religions, but here is their centre. What must be done to attain thereto? Observation and reasoning are not sufficient. In addition to and above all else is intuition. Pythagoras was an adept and an initiate of the highest order. His was the direct vision of the spirit, his the key to the occult sciences and the spiritual world. It was from the primal fount of Truth that he drew his supplies. And as he joined to these transcendent faculties of an intellectual and spiritualized soul, a careful and minute observation of physical nature and a masterly classification of ideas by the aid of his lofty reason, no one could have been better equipped than himself to build up the edifice of the knowledge of the Kosmos.

In truth this edifice was never destroyed. Plato, who took from Pythagoras the whole of his metaphysics, had a complete idea thereof, though he unfolded it with less clearness and precision. The Alexandrine school occupied the upper storeys of the edifice, whilst modern science has taken the ground-floor and strengthened its foundations. Numerous philosophical schools and mystical or religious sects have inhabited its many chambers. No philosophy, however, has yet embraced the whole of it. It is this whole I have endeavoured to reveal here in all its harmony and unity.

THE END

Printed in the United States
6663